Stalking the Power of Boredom

Stalking the Power of Boredom

FINDING AND FOLLOWING THE YELLOW BRICK ROAD OF YOUR LIFE

David B. LeMaster

Table of Contents

Acknowledgements

Compressing flashes of insight and pearls of wisdom into word-containers within the narrow lines of language is difficult. At times it seemed dang near impossible! Certainly this book would have been impossible without the encouragement and dedicated help of a few precious friends I have come to know along The Way.

For endless encouragement and tireless feedback from my patient wife Beverly, there are simply no words to express my gratitude. In addition, I wish to thank my dear friend Linda who helped in my motivational and inspirational difficulties time and again. For giving no quarter to my clueless grammatical trespasses, I owe a great deal to my friend Sandy. I also want to thank my brother Jonathan, whose letter of support kept me going during a low period.

Finally, I would be seriously remiss if I did not also acknowledge the boundless help from those dear friends, loved ones, and guardian spirits on the other side guiding me and this dance of "controlled folly."

I dedicate this book to Marie:
mother, friend, teacher, and fellow Truth-seeker
now roving the stars.

LIFE

"I am that deep hunger
for More.
Within ever-clamoring cells;
more food, more fuel for the living fires.
More air to suck down in great tidal gulps,
to fill tender, pink lungs.
More fire!

I am the unquenchable thirst of the desert grass
waiting for sweet summer rains.
I am the cold seed, in dark soil,
dreaming spring.

I am the rut;
your masculine hunger for sex,
and the feminine longing
for little ones to hold and nurture.

Ever I seek more containers,
more vessels to fill with my lust;
my lust for living!

More wings carving the wind.
More leaves drinking sunlight.
More delicate nets of sparking nerves,
comparing, contrasting, erupting new ideas.

I am that voracious, gnawing, hunger
of the expanding Cosmos
seeking more, ever more,
in all conceivable ways,
to BE!

.

Feast now those delicate blinking eyes
on the glorious light
spraying over this magnificent planet.
Feel the trembling potential of your precious days
to focus the holy light of awareness anew.
Rejoice in this hungry dance of Us becoming.

I am Life!"

Introduction

"The mass of men lead lives of quiet desperation..."
HENRY DAVID THOREAU

So, how bored are you?

Something within you triggered the impulse to reach out and open this book. What was that? What is this hunger for MORE in all of us that pushes us forward? Where does it come from? Could it be that our aversion to being bored goes much deeper and has more profound implications than you ever dreamed? I believe so. In fact, I believe the expanding Universe itself seeks expansion through each of us, but I will elaborate on why this is so a little later.

For now, let's assume that some quiet force prodded you to pick up this book as a means for universal expansion. It is the same force which has relentlessly prodded me for years to write it. As we all know, sometimes this internal prodding by feelings of boredom can be quite unpleasant. As a farm boy I learned the utility of applying an electric cattle prod to the rear end of eighteen-hundred-pound steers to get them into a cattle truck. It seems at times the Universe uses the cattle prod of boredom to get us moving toward our path.

This path, which I refer to in this book as your "Yellow Brick Road," is perhaps the most important discovery you can make in your finite life.

There is a hunter/seeker within us all and my purpose here is to help you recognize this and use the subtle (and not so subtle) signs of boredom to help you on <u>your way</u>. As you will see, by "your way" I mean your divine path in this fleeting, precious life toward MORE. This is a sacred journey made for your steps alone and deep down you have always known this. What you likely have not realized is the importance your feelings of boredom can play guiding you onto and along this path. Perhaps it's time for you to start stalking this strange and rather elusive feeling that has pestered you all your life.

I have found both an important message as well as unfathomable power hidden beneath the irritating discomfort of boredom. I will share with you this startling message and how the very meaning of life, YOUR LIFE, is concealed there. However, first let's look a little closer at this feeling we either tend to run away from, ignore, or indulge in. What do you have to lose but perhaps that quiet feeling of desperation most feel within lives lived far from their Yellow Brick Roads?

CHAPTER 1

Boredom/ A Personal Perspective

"Boredom is the conviction that you can't change...
...the shriek of unused capacities."
SAUL BELLOW

What exactly is boredom? Although everyone seems to know when they are feeling bored, it is rather difficult to put your finger on just what this feeling is. Each of us might feel the tentacles of boredom differently. My wife tells me her boredom feels like a subtle sadness. For me, boredom creeps in like an anxious hunger, which can develop into the panic of a caged hawk. Perhaps you feel boredom as the quiet desperation I mentioned before, seeping like a cold fog and blocking the sunshine in your life. A friend of mine recently posted on Facebook she was feeling, *"crippling, crippling boredom."* No matter how we feel when we are bored, we all invariably seek to avoid it. Are you curious, as I was, where this feeling comes from and what it really means?

We all have experienced the dark side effects of boredom. Have you ever eaten and drunk to excess or taken mind-spinning drugs in an attempt to escape from boredom's clutches? I certainly have. Or have you ever squandered hours shopping for things you didn't need, taken vacations you couldn't afford, or fallen into regrettable relationships all out of boredom? Perhaps you frequently work yourself to exhaustion trying to keep boredom at bay. After some reflection I saw that boredom has probably resulted in more trouble and heartache than all the bloody wars of history! For that matter, I would even bet some of these wars were actually started out of reactions to boredom!

Few realize, however, how the power of boredom can act as a positive force. The hunger of boredom, mixed with curiosity, has driven countless individuals to do amazing things. This interesting relationship between boredom and curiosity is something that I will discuss later. No doubt boredom along with a powerful curiosity played an important role motivating explorers such as James Cook and Magellan to push back the boundaries of what was known of the world. Obviously it was this same mix driving the Wright brothers into the sky and even propelling us to reach out into the dark, cold expanse of space. Artists and musicians, bored with what has been already done, continually push into whole new levels of creativity. This hunger for more, for different, for expanded horizons, is deep within our very core and I will show, even life itself. Humans obviously hate being bored and we will do just about anything to avoid its grasp. Indeed, the most serious punishment society can give a person, short of lethal injection, is locking them up in solitary confinement for the experience of ultimate, unrelenting boredom.

Like most of you I have struggled with periods of boredom all my life. I recall many years ago, sitting behind the wheel of an old VW Beetle (no radio or music) bored out of my flipping mind driving slowly across the painful flatness of Nebraska and Kansas. Then there was the period of time when I worked nights on an assembly line dealing with an endless stream of automatic transmissions. But, I suppose the worst – just by their sheer immensity – were the many years I sat within rows on hard desks doing time in the public education system under flickering fluorescent bulbs. Boredom! I hated it and did everything I could to avoid its tight leash. I remember making quite a few trips to the principal's office due to seeking ways to relieve classroom boredom.

We humans are not alone in feeling the pain of boredom. From a lifetime spent taking care of animals of one kind or another, I know boredom is definitely not exclusively a human problem. Dogs I have owned have been able to telepathically project waves of their bored discontent, without ever making a sound, as I worked at my computer. Then there's the zoo experience. If you have walked among the cages, and had even a gram of sensitivity, I am sure you've witnessed the intense levels of boredom of the inmates. Who can say which is worse to watch, the pacing big cats, or the dark, vacant stares of the great apes? These caged intelligent animals literally reek of boredom. So, what's within them, and us, which is being bored and longing for more?

I have now come to see boredom as an expression of soul hunger. It is a hunger for more stimulation, for more and different input and a more complete expression of the self. The hunger produced by boredom can result in either good or bad consequences depending upon how it's handled. Of course, this is true when dealing with any power. Looking back over my life I realized boredom has been a powerful unconscious and unsuspected motivating force. For me this force, not consciously labeled and being only vaguely felt, tended to seep in as a building irritation, growing stronger until a breaking point was reached. (*Has this been true for you as well?*) It is at this breaking point that action, right or wrong, was usually taken. After dealing over decades with the frequent catastrophic outcomes produced by this process of trial and error, I became more alert to the sharp-pointed proddings of boredom. Eventually, I even learned to cautiously accept its tenacious growth while watching carefully the internal pressure gauges to my "boredom boiler." In short, I've come to appreciate and respect the awesome power of boredom in affecting my life experience.

Boredom has pushed me into many new experiences, from jobs to relationships. This hunger for more lifted me into the skies as a pilot and led me to wander far from home and family. I spent years exploring wild, lonesome country from the frozen Arctic to the sunbaked deserts. The most important consequence of boredom's power for me was when it pushed me into college after the mind-numbing boredom of assembly line work. I had sworn never to be trapped within a classroom again after the hell of high school. (Little did I know that one day, because of this decision, I would go back into high school as a science teacher!)

Far down life's trail, beyond college and graduate school, after many years of trying to understand the workings of the Universe, I had to eventually abandon the soul-less explanations of science. Likewise, the security of my religious training of youth was dropped. Something deep within me became both bored and dissatisfied with these accepted ways of looking at life. I knew there was much more going on and felt this MORE was calling me. After making countless mistakes in the process I finally began to listen more attentively when my soul became bored. There seemed to be a power brooding beneath my boredom and I learned it had best not be ignored.

As happens to most seekers, perhaps even you, there was a dark period when I reached a kind of breaking point. An explosive pressure had built up inside from my desperation to understand the meaning of this wild, unruly thing called "life," the Universe, and the whole point of the game. It was only then, alone by a campfire on the side of an Idaho mountain, that a profound realization concerning the power behind boredom came to me.

It was clear that the hand-me-down, dogmatic beliefs of religion were flawed. Yet, it was just as clear that the cold, mechanistic model of science was equally wrong. The one absolute I saw clearly was the existence of an overwhelming pressure within me and all life to push out, expand, and become more. Similarly, there also seemed to be a universal aversion to confinement or any restriction of this freedom to express and become. It struck me that even the physical universe was itself expanding, faster than the speed of light, becoming MORE! What was this all about? Could there be a relationship between our expanding universe, the evolutionary thrust of life, and the deep aversion to confinement and boredom by all intelligent creatures? Could this "Power of Boredom," as I came to call it, be linked even to the creative, living, force we humans call "God?" Likewise, was there also a relationship between the bore-dom of my soul starving for MORE and the meaning of life?

At some point as a child I remember becoming aware of this ultimate question; *"What is the meaning of Life?"* In my innocence I considered this to be an excellent question, and one I hoped eventually to answer. Being something of a "hick," I didn't realize until college this question was actually considered a sort of joke within our culture. There seemed to be an underly-ing assumption that there really is no purpose to this madness called "life." For reasons I can't explain, even as an adult I still considered the quest for life's meaning to be valid and something I intended to know. (Do you secretly feel this way too?) One thing I discovered about life's meaning was there was a price for this knowledge and this price required giving up many cherished beliefs. This requisite is necessary for any bold seeker to claim the power such knowledge contains.

To comprehend the power I am speaking of, and to follow my suggestions for using it, you might have to give up the following:

- *Some cherished core beliefs concerning the nature of reality and the Universe.*
- *Some deeply programmed beliefs about the nature of "God."*
- *Common misconceptions about the meaning of life in general and your life in particular.*
- *A sense of having plenty of time to figure this all out.*

For many people it seems these costs are simply too high. Change at such a deep level is often overwhelming and few want to rock the boat holding their beloved beliefs, even though most of these were inherited. However, a tsunami wave of change in our understanding of what we call "reality," and our rela-tionship to the Universe, has been breaking upon us in recent years. More and more people are rejecting the handed-down dogma of the past and are eagerly embracing a more positive, intelligent, and expansive view of their place in the

Cosmos. It is for this upwelling of adventurous souls now on our planet (and arriving daily) that this book is written.

One of the most amazing facts I ever heard was a quote by the renowned physicist, Richard Feynman, concerning the latent power within the apparent black emptiness of outer space. According to the late Dr. Feynman, within just one cubic meter of space there exists enough energy to boil all the water of all the oceans on earth! This potential energy source is within the folds of space called the "Zero Point Field." Scientists all over the world are now trying to understand the implications of this energy field and how to access it. Even though the Zero Point Field has been conclusively proven to exist, we simply do not have the technology yet to tap into this incredible power supply.

The book you now hold in your hands is about an even more powerful field of unexpected energy that you can tap into. _This is the latent power within the apparent emptiness of boredom or discontent._ This force, which I am calling the "Power of Boredom," is right here within and around you and, unlike the quantum power of the Zero Point Field, needs no super technology to be used.

"_Outrageous_," you are probably saying to yourself. "_Must be some kind of a sales gimmick_," you think. Well, I certainly understand your skepticism, especially in this time where we are hit almost daily with another plan to "Get Rich Quick," or "Easy Enlightenment for Dummies." So, how could there be any power hidden within or behind the times when you are feeling bored out of your mind? This is exactly what I want to tell you about, but the story is not something I can explain quickly. It has taken me the better part of four decades to put the pieces of this puzzle together and prove this power to myself. So it will take you some time, attention, and a bit of imagination to learn about this power of which I am speaking. In addition, it will then require focused application to use this latent force in transforming your life. "Why should you do this?" Because this power can literally lift you free from the ruts of monotony and the dark swamps of "quiet desperation" into a life of magical adventure!

This process of being a hungry hunter stalking your path of good can be applied by anyone. All that is required is having an open mind and being able to maintain a certain level of alert tenaciousness. Even though the philosophy I am putting forth challenges many traditional views held in both scientific and religious circles, it doesn't matter if you consider yourself a Baptist or a Buddhist. The Universe, and the power behind It, really doesn't care. Skilled hunters come in all shapes, sizes, and denominations. What matters is your intent to have a richer and more adventurous life experience.

So I now encourage you to come along with me as I describe this pervasive power just beneath your feelings of boredom and how you can use it to transform your life. In the process I will also share with you the mind-blowing connection of boredom's relationship on the age-old question of the "meaning of life" and even the nature of "God." The clock is ticking, the sand is pouring through the hourglass, and it's time to find your Yellow Brick Road and hunt bigger game. The question is, *"What do you have to lose, besides your shrieking boredom?"*

CHAPTER 2

Waiting

Waiting
"Serene, I fold my hands and wait,
Nor care for wind, nor tide, nor sea;
I rave no more 'gainst time or fate,
For lo! my own shall come to me.
I stay my haste, I make delays,
For what avails this eager pace?
I stand amid the eternal ways,
And what is mine shall know my face...."

JOHN BURROUGHS

When I was around 10 years old our family moved to a farm in Kentucky. This was an old, rundown farm so the move resulted in years of hard work for my siblings and me. Yet, I was overjoyed. Now I had more "wander-room," and wander the fields and wooded hills I did. Through my teenage years I walked, stalked, hunted, and worked over pretty much every square foot of this and the adjoining farmlands. One of the most important skills I learned during these formative years was how to hunt, and it was the wild, uncooperative animals that eventually taught me the skill and importance of waiting.

Having received a new .22 caliber rifle for my 12th birthday, that fall I enthusiastically took to the woods hunting squirrels. It was a total disaster. During that hunting season, morning after morning, I would go and thrash about the woods chasing after the sounds and glimpses of those pesky, chattering, nut-eating rodents. They easily avoided danger by jumping from branch to branch, and I seldom got even a good look at one, let alone a clear shot. My father trained me to be very precise in my shooting, letting me know that "head shots" were what was expected. He himself was a serious marksman who shot competitively for the Kentucky State Rifle Team. A powerful man with many years of target shooting behind him, he was an excellent instructor. Yet inexplicably, he showed little interest in going out into the woods to teach me how to hunt those scampering squirrels. This confused me for years before I eventually realized the reason. He had been involved with too much ugly killing during the war in Germany. He simply could not bring himself to shoot another warm-blooded thing. However, all I knew at the time was my embarrassment as I trudged empty-handed each morning back to the old brick farmhouse to start my chores. Near the end of that season I eventually did manage to shoot one squirrel, who was obviously old, very deaf, and seriously unlucky. The sad truth was I had no idea how to hunt, and more to the point, no patience for waiting at all.

Being a young, highly energized boy I had "issues" with locked-down classroom time in school. One of the kinder terms used by my teachers to describe my behavior on report cards was "Hyperactive." If I were a middle-school student today I am sure the school nurse would have me on a steady IV drip of Ritalin or some other A.D.D. drug! It was an incredible struggle for me to sit still under flickering fluorescent lights within those square classroom walls. Eventually, it was the squirrels, and not my irritated teachers, who taught me the benefits of patience and how to wait quietly for extended periods. As hunting seasons came and went over the years, I became an increasingly effective hunter through learning well the skill of alert patience. Before this could happen, however, I had to come to terms with the beast of boredom.

There is an important connection between waiting and boredom that I learned sitting in the cool, green Kentucky woods those many mornings ago. It was a personal revelation that I could eventually wait for long stretches of time without a trace of boredom. Yet, this was not the case during those first few seasons of squirrel hunting. Sitting, waiting against the base of a tree for perhaps ten minutes was about all I could handle at a time. By then I usually became so thoroughly bored I would get up and move to another location. Of course, when I did every animal in the forest then knew I was there and either vacated the area or froze quietly until this thrashing boy had passed on by. The problem centered upon not appreciating the importance of waiting, and having little idea what specifically I was waiting for. Without these two important pieces, my monkey-mind became bored and quickly began to think of ways to get "un-bored." Because of my poor performance those first couple years of hunting, I eventually grasped the importance of waiting and I began to understand that what I was waiting for were "signs."

The good hunter is very keyed into the "signs" of his prey and their behavior. Over time the hunter must learn the various sounds and other evidence the game might make or leave behind. I eventually learned to detect the sound of a squirrel cutting on a nut, the soft patter of the nut pieces falling though the damp morning leaves, or the faint sound of a squirrel's small claws on tree bark. This, of course, might seem obvious and easy to someone who has not actually waited in the morning twilight as the forest awakens. But in Kentucky forest reality, screaming blue jays, bellowing cows, buzzing insects in your ears, and maybe even a passing jet, continually masked over the gentle squirrel sounds. Once I learned to recognize the signs I was after, I could sit quietly for hours, often with eyes closed, filtering out the extraneous sounds around me in the woods, picking out those delicate auditory signs of a squirrel nearby. For a very squirmy, "ants-in-your-pants" young boy, this was a profound revelation indeed!

For our purposes here, the point I want to emphasize is that <u>once you know what you are waiting for, and how to identify the signs you're after, it is much easier to wait for extended periods by focusing intently for these signs.</u> Moving now into a much larger arena, these are also the critical skills necessary to stalk and harness the latent power of your boredom to transform your life. I believe you must learn to think and act like a hunter.

Some of you are surely thinking now; "*I am not a hunter and have no interest in becoming one.*" Well, I would strongly disagree with you. We are all hunters in some capacity. When you are looking for that perfect job or the ideal mate, you are hunting. We hunt when we shop for our houses, cars, and the best cell phone data plan. Even when, or I should say, *especially when* you are seeking a deeper connection with Spirit, perhaps with enlightenment the goal, you are hunting.

It is my firm belief that we are all born to hunt and ultimately the prey we are invariably stalking is our "good." Most, however, seem completely unconscious of this and so hunt their good very poorly, as I did thrashing about in the woods. <u>To hunt effectively in life, for whatever it is that you are seeking, you must be able to wait in stillness, identifying the signs within the noisy forest of your life, and then stalk the power beneath your boredom providing those signs</u>. In short, you need to learn how to wait and recognize the signs of what you are waiting for.

In our fast-paced culture "waiting" is the last thing most of us want to do; therefore, at the first hint of "boredom," we jump and move as I did before I learned to hunt effectively. There is a very important underlying assumption within this hunting metaphor that could easily be missed. This assumption, or understanding, took a long time for me to grasp and it may end up being the same for you. At any rate, I feel it is important to at least plant the seed here so you might better understand just what I am speaking about. The assumption, which you must eventually come to verify for yourself, is this:

> *There is an intelligent power seeking to express Itself more fully through your life and it is critical that you learn to wait, listen for, and follow the signs It provides pointing The Way.*

Feelings of boredom, or even mild discontent, are important "signs" not to be dismissed. Because of this a good hunter must thoroughly understand the nature of these signs and interpret them much differently than they may have while growing up. I want now to revisit this thing we have learned to call "boredom." What exactly is it and what does it mean?

Boredom seems primarily to be a mental reaction to perceived unproductive and un-stimulating time. It comes in many subtle flavors and in all shapes and sizes. Basically, I see it as a feeling that there is MORE, and a hunger to experience it.

For example, it could be you are bored with your job, and this kind of boredom could be either mild or severe depending on your situation. It might just be a minor irritation in the back of your mind that the work you are doing is not very fulfilling. Sure, for now it's paying the bills, but you feel deep inside there is so much more out there waiting for you. At some point in our lives most of us have had this kind of boredom. As we know, the problem with this type of nagging boredom is this feeling can dangerously intensify over time. After sticking with the same boring job for many years with a building irritation, you could approach the edge of "going postal." Over time the pressure builds and builds until insane or violent actions might even be taken. Perhaps more commonly, the fear of change holds the bored individual back until something inside withers away as they eventually give up, resigning themselves to the graveyard spiral toward death.

As mentioned before, I have come to see boredom as a kind of hunger. For example, you could just have "the munchies," and would like to find a different snack. At the other end of the scale there is the type of hunger after being lost in the wilderness for weeks. This type of intense hunger is the feeling of your belly button rubbing against your backbone and is on a whole different level. Well, boredom can be like this. It can be merely a subtle desire for some kind of change from where you are, or what you are watching on TV, to a bone-gnawing boredom eating at you day and night relentlessly urging you to make some change, perhaps even a desperate or dangerous one.

The problem for many of us is that we tend to deal with boredom like an oyster deals with a grain of sand in its shell. We frequently just coat over this irritating boring aspect in our lives, like the layers of pearl the oyster uses covering the grain of sand, trying to make it tolerable. Unfortunately, the underlying boredom, the irritation, remains and grows ever more difficult to ignore. A term that has been used for the type of boredom I am talking about here is *"divine discontent."* There is something in you unable to find contentment with who you are, where you are, or what you're doing and your soul desperately yearns for something different. Possibly it is a new location, a more fulfilling relationship, or just a new direction to your life. You feel it eating at you, like a throbbing toothache, screaming for change.

Serious problems are frequently created when we mindlessly, unconsciously, try to alleviate this pervasive boredom with alcohol, drugs, food, or just random, desperate change (for example, someone who bounces from one bad relationship into another.) Such behaviors may distract you for a time, but they don't really feed that deep hunger. In fact, they eventually just dig you deeper and deeper into the dark, damp pit of soul-boredom. Through my work as an emergency medic I have seen the effects of this too many times. When a person's soul-boredom is handled in these ways, I have come to see how it often leads eventually to some form of suicide, either fast or slow. Mr. Thoreau summed up this type of living very well in his quote about most leading lives *"...of quiet desperation."*

Another aspect concerning the hunger of boredom is that it's cumulative, building over time. For me this building is felt as a kind of tension and I now see it being similar to the tension created when drawing back an arrow in a bow. Returning again to our hunting example, imagine you are waiting patiently for the perfect shot at your game as it moves cautiously through the trees and brush. You begin to slowly draw the bowstring against the nock of your arrow, feeling in your arms the building tension. If you grow impatient with this tension and release prematurely, your arrow will lack power and fall short, or perhaps hit brush and be deflected. However, if you draw the string of your bow to full tension too early, your arm and fingers will grow weary, start shaking, and once again, your shot will miss. To make your best shot you must be conscious of the building tension and time the draw so that the bowstring touches your cheek just at the moment the game steps into the clearing.

I imagine some of you thinking now, *"What the heck does shooting an arrow at, say a deer, have to do with me getting out of this boring job situation or into a healthier relationship?"* As I have said before, <u>we are all hunters and what we are hunting is our good</u>, whatever that might be. We each feel there is more waiting for us: more to be, more to do and more to have. The question is then, "How do I navigate from my current (boring/unsatisfying) situation to that MORE?" We need to somehow see THE WAY out of the current situation and then have enough energy to move toward that good. In short, we need both <u>vision</u> and <u>power</u>.

Obviously, in the above analogy, the deer slipping through the brush represents your good. You know it is out there, you can feel it, but from your current vantage point you just can't see the way of getting it. In this situation your hunger for more, indicated by feelings of boredom, increases. As this tension of boredom builds, like the tension of the string in the hunter's bow, most can't withstand the pressure and find some way to relieve it (alcohol, food, TV, sex, domestic quarrels, etc.). In doing this they waste the latent power concealed within their inner feelings of boredom and, like the hunter who gives up and releases his arrow wildly into the bushes, they go hungry! Timing is critical in both forms of hunting. Windows of opportunity open and we must be alert to catch them and have sufficient power then to act.

Waiting is hard. It is especially hard when you are intensely bored, or hungry in our hunting analogy. When I catch myself becoming irritated with waiting for some sign or signal directing me which way to proceed I make myself think about hunting. At these times I imagine a hungry Inupiaq Eskimo throwing a tantrum around a seal's breathing hole that he has been kneeling next to for hours with his spear. How effective would such a hunter be if he started jumping up and down, stomping around the hole in the ice and screaming for the seal to show itself?

What I am describing here is how your feelings of boredom are not only giving you important information, but beneath these hungry, desperate feelings is the very power you need to access and not waste. You need this power to see the signs and signals pointing The Way.

Sounds crazy, right? Yet I have proved this time and again to work in achieving my "good" and I want you to do so, too. (In a little while I will explain why the entire Universe wants you to as well!)

I want to introduce now the key steps in this process of using this power of boredom even though we have yet to cover all of them in detail:

- <u>First, become aware that you are bored/ dissatisfied with some aspect of your life.</u>
- <u>Second, have at least a general idea of the positive change you desire to take place in your life situation.</u>
- <u>Third, be able to wait without wasting this power while you maintain an alert vigilance for signs and signals.</u>
- <u>Fourth, act boldly at the right time to seize your good.</u>

Although the second step of having some idea of the positive change you want to take place in your life is very useful, I personally don't believe it's essential. There have been periods in my life in which I felt strongly that something had to change, but I really couldn't place my finger on exactly what I wanted. In such situations, where you really don't know in what direction your good lies, just affirm that some greater part of you does and then quietly wait upon signs from Spirit to show you The Way. In my case this has frequently then appeared from a totally unexpected direction. Using our hunting analogy this might be hunting because you are really hungry, but are not focusing upon bagging any certain kind of game. So don't worry if you are initially clueless on the specifics of what your better life should look like. Just be open and willing to follow completely unexpected pathways appearing as you wait with vigilance.

There is a possible misconception about this "waiting" I want to clarify now. The type of waiting I am talking about here is definitely not a kind of resignation or passive. It is actually highly dynamic and I will once again draw a comparison from my experiences hunting. Some hunters do prefer to sit in stands or hidden blinds, waiting for their game to appear. This "ambush" type of hunting can be very effective, but the type of hunting I came to prefer, and that better suits our purposes here, is referred to as "still-hunting." Here the hunter uses both periods of alert waiting along with moving slowly, carefully through the territory. Imagine now for a moment being such a hunter. In a state of intense alertness you wait for long stretches of time and then silently, slowly, move, perhaps only a few steps through the woods before pausing to wait once again. In this type of hunting you are really stalking after your prey as you look, listen, and scan for sign. I have found that such careful stalking along the path, The Way, to your good is very much like this kind of hunting. We now need to explore just what signs you are looking for as you quietly slip along through the wild country of your life.

CHAPTER 3

Signs and Signals Along "The Way"

"In every moment the Great Spirit communicates to all creatures everything they need to know. Through ten thousand billion agents ... through the vast and subtle network of living design beyond the weather, before the wind, the truth is ever being transmitted to this world of form."

KEN CAREY

"... all Nature is pervaded by an interior personalness, infinite in its potentialities of intelligence, responsiveness, and power of expression, and only waiting to be called into activity by our recognition of it."

THOMAS TROWARD

Patience alone is not enough for the hunter. He must also be able to spot and interpret signs and signals of his game. In my life I have been fortunate to hunt with a few excellent hunters. They were a delight to observe as they slipped silently through the forest. These men moved very slowly and quietly as their senses rapidly scanned their environment. They stopped often and long, pausing to listen and feel. Their eyes scanned the ground for prints, hair left on branches, scrape marks, anything indicating the proximity of their game, even noticing smells carried on the morning air. It was always humbling to discover how much they saw and were aware of while I was busy being annoyed by the mosquitoes and sticker bushes! For the hunter on the trail of "better yet to be," detecting signs of which way to move requires the same intense focus.

Perhaps you have become aware, through feelings of inner boredom, of a need for a better job. From what you have read here you now understand the need to wait patiently, not wasting the rising power beneath your boredom with scatter activity. It is during this period of waiting, while maintaining the tension of boredom, when you must be ever alert for signs and signals as you stalk carefully through your days.

"Signs and signals from where?" you might be thinking. This brings us to a very important idea, which might be very challenging for minds programmed within our modern western culture. This certainly was for me! In fact, because of a strong background in science, it took me several decades to finally realize that my core beliefs (programming) about 'reality' were deeply flawed. I had been trained to believe the Universe was a cold, heartless, mindless machine in which incredible accidents of chance accumulated creating this world and the abundant life it contained. Actually this viewpoint is a very recent philosophy linked to the highly successful industrial and scientific revolution of the past few hundred years or so. Looking about you right now you will see endless examples of the effectiveness of this scientific and industrial mind-set. Ink pens, books, computers, telephones, reading glasses, tape, electricity, plastic and steel, are just a few examples around me now. These are good and useful things, and I certainly am not suggesting we go back to a time before all our modern conveniences, especially spell-check computers! However, we have collectively made a huge and erroneous assumption in believing the Universe is merely a mindless machine.

More recent scientific models that you may have heard of, such as quantum physics and string theory, have put huge cracks in the foundations of this belief in a mechanistic Universe. (*I am sure this is a great relief to aboriginal Australians and other indigenous people.*) A more ancient belief system about the nature of reality is one in which we live in a conscious, responsive Universe that awaits only our attention. For indigenous cultures around the world this perspective is an obvious "no brainer." To these people, living in intimate closeness with the Earth, relying on hunting, fishing, and seasonal gathering to sustain their lives, the most obvious thing in the world was that they were involved in a vast, conscious relationship with their environment. The concept of this environment being willing and able to communicate with them through signs, signals, and omens was as apparent as the wind and the rain.

Some years ago when I was struggling with this belief of an aware Universe, I was on an extended float trip down the Yukon River. My wife and I had hurriedly stopped on a sandy island scattered with drift logs as the billowing, black thunder clouds rolled rapidly toward us. Lightning flashed across the river as we quickly unpacked the canoe and set up our tent. While she disappeared into the tent to read, I donned all my rain gear (like a good Boy Scout) and stood on the muddy bank watching the storm come rapidly across the river. The thunder was echoing off the hills as I watched the wind and hard rain move relentlessly toward our camp over the broad river's muddy surface. I remember feeling rather smug since I had read the signs of the impending weather and had stopped and prepared before it could "get us." The storm and hard rain literally came only a dozen feet or so from where I stood on the bank, all decked out in rubberized rain gear. This continued for quite some time before the rain slacked off and eventually stopped, leaving a huge double rainbow. I just stood there trying desperately to not see the obvious message. Somewhat sheepishly, I finally took off the hot and quite dry rain gear.

This event was a major turning point for me at the time, but it is rather difficult to explain why so to others. Such events are complex and highly personal. Its impact had to do with the context of my thoughts at the time, my inner struggle in dealing with a scientific world view which was not fitting what I had been observing in my life, and even the book I was reading at the time;

"The Tao of Physics." I simply could no longer deny that something was trying to get my attention and at the same time, poking a little fun at my Boy-Scout tendencies. I have found my communications with the Universe are often like this, especially the humor part. Likewise, I have learned that they are private conversations and trying to share them usually just invites ridicule.

The many years since that event, like a "doubting Thomas," I slowly went out on the ice of this radical view, testing to see if it would support my weight. The validity of this ongoing communication by the Universe is now no longer a question FOR ME. Through decades of carefully watching for and reading these signs, it has eventually become second nature and something I totally depend upon. I am sure there are some of you, "old souls" who have been around the incarnation block a few times, who will find all of this very funny. You have understood all of this long before birth and take such an ongoing discourse with the Universe as a matter of fact. "What's the big deal?" However, perhaps like some others out there, I was a little slow and needed relentless, remedial instruction in order to take me to the point of finally believing and trusting my intuitive side.

Note above I capitalized "FOR ME" in order to emphasize an important point. The signs, signals, omens that the Universe communicates to you are exclusively for you. Period. They only have meaning for you personally, and can only be interpreted by you in the context of where you are and even what you are thinking about in the moment. Trying to explain your "seeing" to anybody else (as I have learned time and again) is just setting yourself up to appear a total nut case! Just listen quietly to the whispering of the Infinite as it leads you along "The Way" with signs and signals having meaning specifically for you.

Now I need to touch briefly on an ancient concept, which frustratingly, can't really be explained according to the Chinese master, Lao Tzu. This is the philosophy of the "Tao" or simply "The Way." When I discovered the philosophy of Taoism it was like drinking cool spring water in the desert. The idea of balancing opposites, and there being a path of harmonious flow through one's life, resonated deeply inside of me. The best image my western mind can conjure up here to explain "The Way," is the "Yellow Brick Road" from the old classic movie, <u>The Wizard of Oz.</u>

I believe we each have our own Tao or Yellow Brick Road, which is the personal path of potential harmony, winding through the jungles of our individual lives. It is a twisty, narrow road, easily lost, and too often we end up thrashing in the sticker bushes and bogs off either side. However, there is a knowing within us recognizing the instant we stagger out of the muck back upon its golden surface. Things suddenly smooth out and we begin to feel light and hopeful. Occasionally you meet individuals who somehow have locked onto their personal Yellow Brick Roads, and they just shine. These people are full of energy, loving life, as they skip along with their little dog and strange friends. It is tempting to try and duplicate their lifestyle. But we all have our own unique path and it just doesn't work if you try jumping on someone else's harmonious trail. <u>Each has his own individualized path of destiny to fulfill.</u> When I speak therefore of receiving signs and signals along "The Way," I am referring to the unique probability thread weaving through the matrix of time which is yours and yours alone.

As you move through the wilderness of the world seeking your special trail, it is very easy to become disoriented and lost. There are so many choices and directions you can go, how do you decide? On the flickering blue television screens by the hundreds of millions we are shown the things and lives we need to be happy. In the full-bore pursuit of this happiness, based largely upon having both the right "stuff" and tribal security, many end up very far from their path of heart. Some may even appear highly successful in the eyes of the world, but not in the sad, bored eyes of their soul. Maybe you end up working at a job you hate or get stuck in relationships that strangle your spiritual growth and joy in life. <u>Your soul is bored!</u> It wants to get back on that Yellow Brick Road with Toto and the gang, on with the very reason you came here for this life in the first place. As this life-stagnation slowly happens, it is all too common for individuals to become complacent sitting in their festering swamp of boredom. They (we) end up wasting time watching reruns on TV, getting drunk, or finding some other way to briefly relieve the building tension of the boredom and thus wasting its precious power.

One blessing of boredom is the endless ways it has of getting your attention that something needs to change. Over and over the alarm bells keep going off from your soul, wanting to be on its Way. Instead of ignoring these alarms or wasting the power beneath your boredom, I believe you should acquire the methods and mood of a hunter. You must wake up and realize life is a hunt for your "good and plenty."

Assuming the ways of a hunter, you now conserve your power and carefully begin stalking Life*, looking for signs and signals from the Universe. If you are patient and resolute, Life will eventually guide you to your path of destiny. (*Stay tuned and I will explain why the Universe truly wants you to be on your Way.*) As dramatic as this will sound, the destiny-hunting of which I am speaking is literally a matter of life and death; the life and death of your very soul.

During this period of waiting it is vital to understand it is not an idle time to "kick back." The question then becomes, "*Just what should I do then, when I am not sure what to do, while I am waiting for some sign or signal from the Universe?*"

First, as many have pointed out before me, <u>it is important to take little, positive steps</u> as an indication of your intent. Years ago I came up with the following saying during a long, gray period of personal waiting; "*If you don't know what to do, do the dishes.*" Get moving! Clean things up, go over your

---

* Throughout this book I use the words "Universe," "Spirit," "God," "Tao," and "Life" interchangeably all referring to the same vast and indefinable Being of which we are a part. Because of this, all these terms are capitalized.

camping gear, or update your resume. In short, put your house in order. I believe this demonstrates to the Universe that you are serious and ready for a change. This might also mean joining a help group like A.A. or taking a class at night school. Second, <u>you need to constantly work on your LOC, or "Level of Consciousness."</u>

CHAPTER 4

LOC

"Do not strive or seek for heavenly riches in human consciousness. Wait! Wait! Seek a higher level of consciousness: There the Father's treasures are as free as air."
JOEL GOLDSMITH

"[It's] not your aims or your actions [that] are primary, but the state of consciousness out of which they come."
ECKHART TOLLE

Every trained First Responder, EMT, and Paramedic is well acquainted with the term "Level of Consciousness," or simply, "LOC." The constant evaluation of an accident patient's LOC is critical and can be the first indication the patient is in serious trouble even if outside appearances don't indicate much is wrong. In emergency medicine a person's LOC is determined by their comprehension and ability to articulate "person, place, time, and event." This is done by asking the patient questions such as; *"Where are you?" "What happened?" "What's your name?" "What year is it?"* or even *"Who's the president?"* If they just stare at you and mumble something unintelligible, then the "computer" between their ears is likely having an issue.

A common symptom of someone who struck their head in an accident is asking the same question or saying the same thing over and over like a broken record. It is also possible that on the surface they appear totally fine, and are even able to carry on a conversation but, as happened with a patient of mine once, be missing a couple of decades when asked the year. If the LOC of a patient seems to be going downhill while transporting, it could indicate a bruised and swelling brain, or they are slipping into shock. Therefore, continually checking a patient's LOC is vital in emergency medicine. I believe this is also true for those stalking the power of boredom waiting for signs pointing the path to the good they seek.

As we go about our day the constant babble of 'self-talk' can be relentless. It seems that only while in meditation, or when I'm engaged in an activity demanding my total attention, does my mental chatter finally subside. By listening in to this monologue you can often get a sense as to where your LOC is currently, or maybe the direction it's heading. *"Why does this matter?"*

To completely answer that question we would need to travel down a long and convoluted Alice-in-Wonderland rabbit hole. For our purposes here I will just point to that bunny hole by repeating what wisdom teachers have been saying for a long time; *"Your thought stream, and the emotional vibrations produced by this chronic flow, create your reality."*

When I am waiting for guiding signs I frequently monitor my own LOC. You could call this practice, *"checking in with the mystic-medic."* Here your inner medic monitors your thoughts and streaming self-talk determining at just what level your consciousness is hovering. Some examples of what you might hear are: *"How in the world can you afford a bigger home?" "If I get a divorce from this abusive jerk, how will I support my kids?" "Times are tough now and I should just be glad to have this boring job."* Closer to home for me, *"This stuff sounds really crazy; who will even read this book?"* When you listen in with your imaginary stethoscope, it is amazing just how relentless and often self-defeating our thoughts can be. At times my mystic-medic can only let out a deep sigh as it realizes my LOC is dropping through the floor down into a dark, depressing basement!

One steamy July day, when I was a teenager in need of money, I did some grave digging for a small local church. Down in that hot hole I chipped at the clay and rock, inching my way to the required depth. It was summer in Kentucky, and I was drenched with sweat and covered head to toe with sticky brown dust. As I got down closer in the hardpan clay to the six-foot goal, my viewpoint became rather limited as you might imagine. Kneeling down chipping at that bone-dry ground, above me there was only a rectangular slice of hazy summer sky visible. This is a good analogy for how a low LOC restricts the perception of what you see as possible. You can allow your consciousness to literally slide down into the deep, depressing hole that you have dug. Thoughts colored by fear, doubt, self-pity, or guilt will pull you down into that hole, and keep you there, if you let them.

Some years after my grave-digging employment, I was a new pilot in a small Cessna airplane. That blue-bird morning I found myself carving turns 1000 feet above this very same church graveyard. From this elevated vantage point I now had a much broader perspective (it was also a bit cooler). The point here is that as we raise our level of consciousness whole new possibilities become apparent. In short, when you <u>raise your perspective you change your perceptions</u>. This is vital for the hunter of The Way, because thoughts are powerful.

All the way back in 1889 the New Thought pioneer Prentice Mulford wrote the classic book "<u>Thoughts are Things</u>." In the 1930's, just after the Depression, Napoleon Hill expanded upon this theme with the highly popular book, "<u>Think and Grow Rich</u>." Then in 1952 "<u>The Power of Positive Thinking</u>" by Norman Vincent Peale was published. A veritable avalanche of books has been written since then on the importance of controlling your thoughts in order to change your reality. In a more recent book, "<u>The Field</u>," Lynne McTaggart describes many scientific studies which clearly demonstrate the ability of thoughts to affect the outcome of experiments. Can you see now why it's so critical to carefully monitor your thoughts? This is even more so for you who have identified boredom in your lives and are waiting for signs pointing the Way to a more abundant life. When you detect your LOC is dropping, you must take immediate action stopping this mental/emotional backsliding. What sort of actions would these be?

There has been much written on the effectiveness of prayer. There is ample evidence that prayer can and has at times produced miraculous results. However, I think there are inherent problems with some common beliefs surrounding the traditional prayer model and these beliefs can be very difficult to change. Since praying is such a powerful tool for maintaining an elevated LOC, as an effective hunter/stalker along your Yellow Brick Road, you need to be aware of these old, limiting beliefs and how they can actually keep you from your good.

Like many of you, I learned to pray at a young age. These prayers were mostly begging in nature, combined with sincere promises on my part of better behavior when my prayers were answered. As far as effectiveness goes, this seemed a hit or miss proposition, which mostly missed. As I grew older (and more crafty) I learned to get Mary, Jesus, Joseph, the Saints and Apostles, all involved to "intercede" to the great father God (resembling the ancient Norse God, Thor). Again, this did not seem to work very well in terms of results. Much later in life I discovered the practice of making affirmations, creative visualizations, and Science of Mind spiritual mind treatments. The results using these techniques were, and remain, astounding! It was only when I was able to delete the deeply-embedded *"begging a reluctant God"* belief that my praying results dramatically improved. I then had to ask myself, "So what's going on here?"

Most of us have been raised with an "us and them," or victim, mentality. In short, we believe, at a core level, in duality and separation. We have been taught that there is "God" and the "Devil." There is both a "heaven" and a "hell." This duality list goes on and on. Yet, with any deep thinking, you realize this reality paradigm can't be true. All the great mystics on our planet have seen this. An important consequence of there really being, at the deepest level, no

<u>duality or separation within the Universe is that our thoughts and beliefs have a profound power.</u>

Dr. Ernest Holmes spent his life exploring, explaining, and demonstrating this power through the <u>Science of Mind</u> philosophy he developed. His seemingly simplistic phrase, *"Change your thinking, change your life,"* has been the foundation for the so-called, "new thought movement." In a very small nutshell this philosophy boils down to: <u>*"As you think and believe, the Universe will create within form and circumstance."*</u> This is known now as "The Law of Attraction." No doubt many of you have seen the 2006 documentary film, "The Secret," focusing upon this Law. Since then a large cargo ship could be filled with all that's been written concerning the use of this Law. I have no intention in adding to this cargo load. However, I do want to briefly discuss the importance of understanding and using this Universal Law in stalking your good.

For myself, it has been the works of Abraham, by Jerry and Esther Hicks about the Law of Attraction, which have been the most influential. Their books and recordings have helped me understand how I truly live in a vibratory Universe where *"vibes" of a feather flock together*, so to speak. In my previous example concerning prayer, when your prayer is "begging a reluctant God," you are praying from a consciousness of lack. Therefore, it is a vibration of lack which you are projecting. Due to the Law of Attraction, the ever-listening and responsive Universe then matches this vibration with more evidence of lack. Likewise, when you maintain an affirmative mindset, vibrating the frequency of an intensely alert, expectant hunter, stalking your Way, the Universe responds by providing signs and signals for you to follow.

Hopefully, you see clearly now the reason begging prayers are less effective than those affirming your unity with the whole. The reason has to do with the very nature of this system we call "reality." The old religious model we learned is analogous in chemistry to the Bohr model of the atom. In this model the atom was described as being a miniature solar system with tiny electrons orbiting the dense nucleus. This view was useful for a time but was soon found to be much too simplistic. Likewise, the model of a patriarchal God, who may or may not grant favors, is just no longer useful. Unfortunately, this model seems based more upon human psychology and not on any evidence. The prefix "Uni" in the word "Universe" means ONE. This pretty much sums up the misconception. There is only ONE! We are not separate from it. The system, the Universe, started with a singularity (Big Bang) and therefore must be unified in essence. Period.

When you use affirmations, you are affirming this underlying unity along with your rightfully empowered place within It. <u>The Universe then simply responds to Itself, AS YOU.</u> However, when your mindset is one of separation, where you believe you must beg and plead, you are not aligned with the greater Truth/Reality of what is. <u>This is why it is so important, when stalking the trail of your good, to keep your level of consciousness at an elevated, positive frequency as much as possible.</u> When you allow yourself to slip into the "*poor, poor, pitiful me*" mindset, you are just slamming the brakes on the way to your good. Again, the Universe will absolutely agree, due to the Law of Attraction, giving you more of the same.

In science we have learned very well during the past several centuries the importance of aligning ourselves with the laws of nature in order to obtain useful, predictable results. Electricians can't ignore the laws of electricity and hope to wire a house correctly. We are learning now, through the Abraham/Hicks materials and productions such as "The Secret," how alignment with the laws governing the spiritual side of nature is just as important.

This brings us to one of the largest stumbling blocks for me, and perhaps you as well, in this process of hunting for my good. What mystified me for a long time was accepting that the Universe ("God") could and would actually provide this concrete guidance. How would IT know what I was seeking? How is it possible for signals to actually come to me, at times instantaneously, from the world of even inanimate matter? These questions troubled my scientific mind for many years. Who would have thought that a fairly recent scientific understanding would eventually help answer these questions for me? What a deeply _entangled_ ocean of connections we are swimming in!

CHAPTER 5

Entanglement

"I tell you, if these were silent, the very stones would cry out."
LUKE, 19:40

"There is a Universal Wholeness seeking
expression through everything."
ERNEST HOLMES

Just the other morning, a bright, frosty November morning, well over a thousand starlings descended upon our back yard. They were draped like a noisy, vibrating, black blanket over the Russian Olive trees, bowing the slender branches with their collective weight. Even our small birdbath was piled with a rounded, squirmy mass of the feathered varmints as they tried to get a sip of water. As our neighbor went out to start his truck they arose in a chattering, undulating cloud. I remarked to my wife, who was watching the show by the window drinking her coffee, how I wondered what Mr. Shakespeare would have to say about causing this backyard show. She just gave me that "look," and went back to her steaming mug. It was an hour or two later before I realized how this event was 'heaven sent' to help me in my struggles writing this chapter on entanglement.

It is a well-known fact in birding circles that William Shakespeare is to blame for our having European starlings in this country. Back in the 1800's the

American Acclimatization Society decided they should introduce into the U.S. every bird mentioned in Shakespeare's works. So in 1890, and again the following year, Eugene Schiefelin, a local drug manufacturer, released 80 starlings in New York City's Central Park. Just like us, they did quite well here and now it's estimated there are over 200 million members of *Sturnus vulgaris* in the United States! Simple acts can certainly result in profound, unanticipated effects.

I think one of the most important "discoveries" by science in the past hundred years was that of the intense interconnectedness in nature known as "Ecology." Of course the indigenous tribes have intuitively known of this tangled interconnectedness for tens of thousands of years. Only in recent times, however, have we learned just how intricate these connections really are, down even to the molecular level.

Our very bodies are composed of interacting populations of cells whose relationships are not really different than the interacting populations of the various species within a forest ecosystem. The harder science has looked, the deeper this interconnected entanglement appears to go. It is now well accepted in the Life Sciences that even the individual cells of our bodies are in fact composites. They are an aggregation of formerly autonomous organisms (anaerobic bacteria), some even with their own genetic histories, such as the mitochondria. Ecologically, each of us is literally an entangled mess suspended within a dynamically tangled, living web. However, you will soon see, it is really much more complicated than this!

Years ago I ran up against a mental brick wall as I struggled to understand how this thing called "reality" worked. Based upon the old model of reality, what I began experiencing seemed completely insane. To my scientifically-programmed brain it was just crazy that the world of "stuff" around me could act aware and responsive. Yet, I could not deny my perceptual data. The world was giving me signs and signals I could no longer ignore or write off as mere "coincidence." It is one thing to read about gifted individuals such as Edgar Casey, Jane Roberts, and more recently Esther Hicks, receiving channeled information from the 'other side,' and quite another to experience communications of your own. I didn't have a problem accepting that such things were possible; it was just hard to believe they could happen personally to me, in "real time."

I was fortunate in being raised by a strong, intelligent woman who had no problem believing in the unseen world. My mother was quite psychic and often used phrases such as, "*my little friends on the other side said...*" Or this or that object (tree, bush, bird, rock, etc.) "*Spoke to her.*" I loved her dearly, but back then I couldn't buy into her perceptions. Instead, I voraciously focused upon the scientific explanation of Nature. During this time Science was my path to "Truth," and I ended up taking that path as far as I could. Without a doubt, there was (and is) great beauty and power in the discoveries made using the scientific method, but something essential seemed missing. Eventually, over the years, I realized I no longer could buy into the package of assumptions being peddled in the halls of academia. How can you evolve Life, consciousness, a Jesus or a Buddha, from random atomic collisions? Having spent so much of my time wandering and hunting in the wild, I knew in my bones that somehow "It" was alive, all of It! Of course shamans and mystics the world over have been saying this for eons.

Being stuck somewhere in the middle between these two opposing reality views, for years I felt adrift without a solid philosophy. I gradually had to admit something definitely seemed to be trying to communicate with me (*as indicated with my previous story of the rainstorm event while on a canoe trip*). Believe me, the scientist in me put up a good fight, and I tried every which way to explain away the signs and signals I was getting. However, there seemed to be a growing communication pressure from something which I came to call, "IT." Eventually I realized this "IT" was simply the Universe, both the seen and unseen.

The day the bizarreness of this really hit home I was 20 feet up a ladder working on a house construction problem. I was cutting and fitting pieces of sheet aluminum into complex three-dimensional shapes for a house overhang.

On this occasion, every time I thought I had it figured out and started to bend and cut the eight-ft. section of coil stock I became aware of some strong negative signals. Something felt wrong and I was getting resistance. Years before I would not have even noticed these signals and just plowed on ahead, ruining the expensive sheet of aluminum. But at this point of my life, after having made some real whopper mistakes from such "blind-running," I listened. I was now more sensitive and had learned from the many painful lessons which had come from ignoring my intuition. So, after a couple attempts, I stopped, found a long piece of cardboard and took the time to make a model of the piece I needed to make. Sure enough, I discovered I would have bent the sheet backwards.

There are a couple of key points I need to make clear here before I continue. For whatever reason, it seems some individuals reach a point of what might be called "spiritual maturity' in life. The old ways of living and believing no longer work as they become aware of more. Because this "more" won't fit into the old reality model, they are forced to come up with a broader, more inclusive explanation for what they perceive. I now understand this was what I was going through after leaving the Newtonian, mechanistic model of reality behind.

I believe we are currently experiencing a powerful time of change with more individuals going through an accelerated spiritual growth process on the planet than ever before. It is for these individuals, perhaps stuck, as I was between world-views, that I am writing this book. The second point I want to make is that developing lines of communication with the Universe (your "higher self," "guardian angels," "God," whatever) can be tricky. Understand when you begin to open up these lines of communication a highly personal system of "sign language" develops. I have read of some rare individuals reporting they actually hear a guiding voice. However, for me, and others I know, this communication is usually symbolic in nature. It can be much like dream interpretation, which I suppose makes perfect sense.

Returning now to the construction problem, what the heck was going on here? This story is embarrassing in its mundaneness and part of me really didn't want to include it. I mean, why would the Universe ("God") care about some stupid piece of aluminum? I could not deny the validity of the signs of resistance I had gotten; yet I was at a total loss as to why this event was of any importance to the great "IT." Of course wasting a long piece of expensive aluminum trim was important for the homeowner and my boss who had bought it, but why would the Universe give a rat's behind about it? This question kept resurfacing over decades as I experienced countless other examples of such intuitive communication from the supposedly inanimate world. Then I learned about "entanglement."

In my science studies I had gained a basic (very basic) understanding of quantum physics and learned about pairs of electrons doing strange things because they were "entangled." Albert Einstein referred to this as, "*Spooky action at a distance.*" However, it wasn't until much later, when I saw the movie "The Secret," that the explanation to my long-time question hit me between the eyes. Before I tackle entanglement, this is a good place to point out not all scientists are stuck in the "clockwork universe" model of the 1800's. There have been many fascinating studies by researchers in the last 50 years into the interconnected complexity of (assumed) inanimate matter and mind. Lynne McTaggart's book The Field is an excellent review of a number of these paradigm-shaking studies.

Now let's look at this phenomenon of "entanglement," which has been causing a great deal of head scratching among physicists. Briefly, the term is used to describe the ability of particles, such as electrons and photons (*and recently even much larger clumps of matter*), which can INSTANTLY communicate information with one another across, apparently, any distance. The main requirement is that they must have been created together to have this entanglement principle occurring. As I was watching the movie The Secret, a physicist pointed out that, since the entire Universe was created from a singularity at the moment of the Big Bang, all matter in the Universe is potentially entangled! This means, at some level, the matter making up my body and the piece of aluminum I had been working on were entangled, and potentially able to communicate. It was feasible, due to this "spooky" phenomenon of entanglement, that information from inanimate objects could, on some level, be instantaneously communicated to us.

Therefore, my dear mother was not totally off her rocker in her claims the hairbrush "spoke" to her when it was lost under a pile of magazines. A main requirement is you must be sensitive enough, and aware enough, to tap into this ongoing communication from the 'stuff' making up this amazing, entangled Universe.

I do realize that going from the laboratory communication of a pair of spinning electrons, to "speaking hairbrushes" is just a bit of a stretch. Yet the potential for this communication is present at the core of all matter. Who can definitively declare to knowing the boundaries of consciousness? However, this doesn't answer my old question of, "Why would the Universe-as-house-aluminum-trim care which way the job was done even if it had to be redone several more times?" If indeed all matter is entangled, and can even communicate on some level, what difference does it really make how it all plays out?

Eventually, I came to understand that The Universe intends to flow in harmonious patterns. In a few chapters I will attempt to shed some light on this statement, but for now it is important for you to understand an important implication of this. You see, the concept of the "Yellow Brick Road" or the "Tao" does not just apply to you and your boredom. The Way of harmonious flow applies at all levels in this entangled system we call the Universe. To this flow there really are no "important" or "unimportant" doings. There is only "Tao or not Tao," "The Way" or the briar patch beside the road. ALL OF IT is connected or entangled; both the perception and the perceiver. What you will eventually discover by practicing this method I am outlining, like a hunter seeking the path to your individual good, is that ripples of harmony (Tao) from your quest will radiate out and positively affect everything and everyone around you.

When Shakespeare mentioned starlings in his scripts he had no clue of the rippling affect his words would set in motion. Life is like that. The threads shoot out, in every conceivable direction, creating webs of connections from our thoughts, actions, words, and dreams with the ALL. Within this dynamic, aware, responsive Universe we are part of, we must eventually awaken from the childish dream of isolation and become aware participants in this entangled process. To understand what I am saying with this book, and use the power hidden within boredom, you must shift from the outdated model of how the Universe works which we inherited from the 1800's. We know better now. This old model, in which you are a separate, isolated individual needing to apply force to get your needs met, is a myth. We each truly are an integral part of an energetically entangled Universe. The underlying vibrating quality of this system, on a scale defying any human comprehension, is "<u>awareness</u>." This ancient knowledge is nothing new and all the shamanistic cultures of antiquity tapped into this field of permeating intelligence.

Awareness is the key, not only for perceiving the signs and signals directing you back to the Yellow Brick road of your life, but also in understanding the very purpose behind this whole, amazing system. First, however, I want to make sure you understand what I mean when I use the term, "*awareness.*"

"We are mass-energy. Everything is energy. EVERYTHING!"
Movie, <u>The Secret</u>

CHAPTER 6

The Light of Awareness

"Only that day dawns to which we are awake."
Henry David Thoreau

Are you truly awake? So, how aware are you? What the heck is "awareness" anyway? These are questions I have pondered for some time. As a young hunter quietly stalking game, I learned the importance of maintaining a heightened level of awareness. Many times my prey would explosively take off vanishing just as my attention wandered in some daydream. Being a hunter on your path to a more abundant life it is certainly important you maintain a sharp awareness. However, it is critical that you also have some understanding as to what actually is *awareness*. Unfortunately, it is a rather slippery topic to directly grasp and analyze. For me the place I gained true insight into this phenomenon was during meditation practice.

Sitting comfortably, quietly, I center my awareness upon my breathing. I follow the breaths in and out, aware of the rise and fall of my chest. As the brain noise fades I notice my body is slightly rocking with the slow, regular beat of my heart. Gradually, the inner silence deepens and I start noticing "popcorn" thoughts and images sneaking in on the projection screen of my mind. As I stubbornly refocus awareness upon my breathing, they fade slowly back into the vibrating silence. If this is a "good meditation," it feels like 'I' fade away for an indeterminate time leaving only what I can describe as a permeating field of awareness of which I am a vibrating part. Of course, as soon as "I" happen to notice this, I am instantly outside the "field," looking back at it. Then once again I notice my breathing, my heartbeat, and the eagerly-returning thoughts.

According to my wife, the closest she gets to meditation is when she is try-ing to fall asleep at night. She calls the popcorn thoughts "the squirrels" which keep darting and jumping sporadically from one neural branch to the next. Clutching some random thought like a precious nut (*such as, how to change a process at work, the list of chores to get done in the next couple of weeks, letters to write, or what to set out for dinner the next day*) they scamper about. These rogue mental rodent ramblings keep her in a state of agitated alertness defy-ing any drift into relaxing sleep. Since she has become aware of the free reign she previously gave "the squirrels," she now uses this awareness to pivot her consciousness upon the sound of the white noise maker by the bed. Instead of relinquishing control to the chattering thought-squirrels, she has learned to redirect her awareness upon the astringent hum of the machine to quiet them.

There seem to be infinite levels of awareness and it has been difficult for me at times to differentiate "awareness" from "consciousness." I don't think I am alone in having but a vague understanding of the difference between these words. Now I think of consciousness as simply being "awareness squared." In other words, consciousness is a state of being aware that you are aware, compared to just raw awareness. At the moment, some part of you reading these words is aware of the temperature of the room, yet you are probably not "conscious" of this. (*That is, unless the temperature becomes sufficiently uncomfortable for the conscious you to notice.*)

One fascinating example of how we are often aware of much more on an un-conscious level than we realize is when hypnosis is used to take someone back to an event they are unable to recall. During these regressive hypnotic sessions some individuals are able to now relate minute details of the event and even of their surroundings at the time. It is obvious from these studies that some part of us is definitely more aware of what's going on around us than we are usually conscious of. This really can get interesting when the person under hypnosis happens to travel right back through their time in the womb into a completely other lifetime!

In 1980, Dr. Brian Weiss, a Columbia and Yale University trained psychologist, had a client ("Catherine") do just this. At the time, he claimed to have no belief of any kind in reincarnation and was thus very skeptical about the detailed information he received on the former lifetimes of his client. Later, he was able to confirm many elements of Catherine's story searching through public records. Because of this, and many more similar cases of past life regression, Dr. Weiss wrote a series of eight books after first publishing Catherine's story in "Many Lives, Many Masters." These intriguing books clearly support the continuance of human awareness beyond death. My point here is to suggest that there don't seem to be any rigid barriers where the light of our awareness can flow and what we may even become conscious of.

Thinking about pure awareness can be really confusing and, from personal experience, even result in headaches. So let's back up for now and talk about one of my favorite topics, *vision*. I have always been fascinated by the nature of light and the many diverse structures living things have evolved for both receiving and decoding the flood of information coming from our illuminated world. A little later I will slip quietly around to the back door of this perplexing yet important concept of "awareness."

On a recent checkup with the eye doctor I learned the optic nerve running from the back of my eye's retina to the brain has over a million nerve fibers! *(In my mind I struggled trying to imagine a phone cable with a million tiny wires fitting within my eye socket.)* He went on to explain there were actually many more nerves than this running from the individual receptor cells (the rods and cones) within the retina before joining that large optic nerve. These specialized light-sensitive cells are arranged in a thin coating along the curved retinal wall very much like a curved movie screen. The light images from the world outside are focused upon this layer of sensitive cells by the flexible lens at the front of the eye. They in turn, after being stimulated by the incoming light image, fire off a steady stream of electric neural pulses to the brain centers for interpretation. This electrical transmission is done in Morse code fashion, literally a series of "dots" and "dashes." This ongoing visual transmission of information happens over and over (*and is happening as you read this*), literally without a conscious thought. It is only due to this complex photochemical-neural interplay that I am able to have awareness of a vibrant desert sunset, or the luminous stellar arc of the Milky Way overhead. How miraculous is our eye's ability to capture and focus the reflected light of the world upon that thin layer of photosensitive cells!

What is pertinent here, in our backdoor discussion on awareness, is the shocking truth that what you think you "see" is not reality at all, or at least the complete picture. Due to the processing and filtering taking place, first within the retina, and then within the visual cortex of the brain, what you actually "see" is a pixilated, rough facsimile of "reality." Who knows what information has been hurriedly left out and is lying in piles on the editing room floor? This may even explain how certain sensitive individuals are able to see colorful auras, or deceased family members from the other side wanting to pass on a message. It is obvious that awareness is indeed relative to the one perceiving.

Having studied and taught within the life sciences for many years, I tend to view "awareness" from a much broader perspective than most. For example, when I speak of "awareness" I am including such things as:

The obvious awareness expressed by the countless microscopic protozoans zipping and dancing on their private missions in the puddles and swamps of, say, Florida,

The tracking of the sun's position in the sky by Arctic buttercup flowers as they twist their parabolic flower heads in order to focus the radiant warmth upon developing seed embryos,

The awareness of the changing ratio of daylight to dark by plants and migrating birds physically, behaviorally, and metabolically preparing for the changing seasons,

The awareness of "self" versus "non-self" by burly white blood cells roving in packs through our blood vessels looking for invaders.

This list is infinite and with any focused study of living things it becomes obvious that "awareness," in some capacity, is a characteristic of all life. The mistake most make is to think of awareness only in human terms. It is also important to understand I am not saying that white blood cells and the buttercup flowers are necessarily "conscious." In addition, I don't think you can say that the entangled electrons, aluminum siding, or my mother's hairbrush in the last chapter are truly "aware." Perhaps another way to view these instances would be to say the objects were "linked" by some instantaneous quantum flow of information. Living systems such as plankton, starfish, and great white sharks are vastly more energetically aware and responsive. What I find very interesting is that awareness and responsiveness among even so-called "lower" forms of life goes much farther than formerly thought.

Cleveland Backster made astonishing discoveries concerning plant awareness in the 1960's. He was working at the time for the CIA as an Interrogation Specialist refining the use of the polygraph or "lie detector" machine. Quite by accident he found that plants responded strongly on a polygraph machine to both his thoughts and actions, specifically those concerning injury to the plant or even other life forms! He termed this type of awareness 'primary perception,' and has worked over the ensuing decades to refine his techniques and the scope of his studies. Although the scientific community has not exactly embraced his research, his findings have been reproduced in numerous labs around the world and even on an episode of the television show "Myth Busters." However, rather than giving a summary of this fascinating work, I merely wish to point out how this quality we call "awareness" is much broader and pervasive than we were led to believe.

All of us are each immersed in a pulsing sea of energetic information. Sound waves, heat radiation, sunlight, and smells swirl around us. The degree to which we are aware of these various modalities of information, riding upon this surging energetic sea, strongly determines the depth and quality of our lives. It is difficult for me to imagine a life without the ability to see a mountain sunrise, smell a fresh-cut lawn, or hear the sweet song of a meadowlark in the spring. However, I often wonder about all the other incoming data I must be missing.

It was actually only a short time ago that we humans defined our "reality" solely by what we could physically see, hear, taste, smell, and touch. With the breakthroughs in scientific instrumentation over the past few centuries we have discovered that the information perceived with our physical senses was only a thin, microscopic slice of the vibrating ocean surrounding and constantly washing over us undetected. There was just so much more going on which we were totally unaware of. Pigeon poop, of all things, is my favorite example for pointing this out.

Back in 1964 a couple of young scientists working for the Bell Labs in New Jersey were baffled by a radio noise problem they couldn't explain. At the time they were involved in building ultra-sensitive microwave receivers for use in radio astronomy. This electronic noise they were picking up with their antenna was of extremely low energy, yet it seemed to be coming from every direction. At one point they thought the noise was from New York City itself, but on examining their microwave antenna on the roof, they discovered it was thickly covered with pigeon droppings. Assuming they found the cause for their background noise, they cleaned up the antenna and (sadly) shot the birds. Yet inexplicably, the noise remained. Eventually it was discovered that the electronic noise they were picking up was actually the background radiation left over from the Big Bang! They had literally picked up the microwave echo from the creation of the Universe still reverberating from all points in the sky. For this inadvertent discovery they were eventually awarded the Nobel Prize.

Evidence gained from our best science strongly supports the theory our Universe started out as an infinitesimally small point, a singularity, around 13.6 billion years ago with what has been called, the "Big Bang." (*Of course this was, in reality, a totally silent event since, not only was there no medium for the propagation of sound waves, there was not even any space in which such a medium could exist!*) The mind-blowing point here is that <u>EVERY THING</u> in the universe, from galaxies to gazelles, from stars to starfish, from electrons to elephants, can be traced back to that tiny singularity, much smaller than the period at the end of this sentence. Although this theory of creation is now accepted by science, at first it was not. Albert Einstein, for one, strongly believed the Universe was a static system, which had always been and would always be. Attempting to mathematically prove this view he later confessed to "*making the biggest mistake of my life.*" His mistake was when he used a mathematical 'fudge-factor' in order to keep the pesky universe from undergoing any expansion in his calculations. The subsequent discovery of the Big Bang singularity was, using the term of a former vice president, a very "inconvenient truth."

Truth can be like that. It can quietly seep in through the cracks, like a propane leak, threatening to blow apart our deepest and most cherished beliefs. The problem with becoming more aware is that the more data you obtain, the more difficult it can become fitting it all into our former, hand-me-down models of understanding. Just like Einstein, most of us create numerous "fudge factors" in order to keep our perceived "reality" fitting neatly within our "old wine skins." But what is the full truth about the nature of "awareness?" When I reflected on this question over the years, I couldn't recall this important topic ever being addressed in my many years of science education. It was only after my "old wine skin" models of reality had totally failed me that I began to think hard and long about this difficult to grasp topic.

My thinking eventually brought me to the questions, "*What exactly is awareness, and from where did this quality come?*"

The image or analogy, which eventually surfaced was of awareness being a kind of "light." When we turn our awareness toward something it's as if we are shining a light upon it. This light of awareness we are shining then bounces from the object of our attention and the reflected image is analyzed (in much the same manner as happens with light by our physical eyes). But with this 'light,' the analysis is done on deeper levels and likely not just those contained within our brains.

For example, when you shine this so-called "flashlight of awareness" upon the face of a friend, loved one, or even your favorite pet, you can sense if they are troubled or happy. The more sensitive you become, the more information you can perceive with this light, even to the extent that you may be able to feel the emotional energy of someone who has just left the room before you entered. The point here is that awareness is a fluid quality whose level can be quite different between one individual and the next, or even one hour to the next. Its tides seem to come and go.

From my meditation experiences I discovered that even though awareness can seem to ebb and flow like tides through us, deep down there is a baseline field which seems absolute and eternal. The most profound thing I can say about awareness is it simply IS. I believe this permeating field of awareness, which I have sensed in deep meditation, or out in the wilderness, is the "Presence" Eckhart Tolle speaks of in his book, The Power of Now. This "Presence," this field of awareness, simply IS. Therefore, my old question as to where awareness comes from is pointless. Awareness appears to be the ground state of the Universe, much like the omnipresent radiation echo of the Big Bang singularity.

Over time I saw a tremendously important connection between awareness, "God," and the meaning behind this glorious wildness called "Life." It is within this connection, or actually because of it, that a profound power exists within your boredom just waiting to be tapped into. I will explain this fully in the next chapter, but for now just realize the essential starting point for understanding this connection is knowing <u>awareness is an intrinsic attribute of, not only life in general, but of the whole system as well</u>.

Science would have us believe "awareness" just sort of happened, like life, from random chemical collisions. Many religions propose an outside directing intelligence from another realm called "heaven." For me it makes more sense to just accept, as so many indigenous peoples around the planet have for eons, that Life is a property of the Universe and the whole system is very much aware (or quantum-connected) on some level. The recent discoveries from quantum physics such as Entanglement and the Zero Point Field point in this direction of thought as well.

As I pointed out earlier, our current scientific understanding is that the Universe started out from a singularity, smaller than an atom, with the Big Bang. Looking around now, some 13.6 billion years after this event, we find an amazing diversity of life, on one planet at least, all having the special quality called "awareness." One species, humans, has even achieved various levels of "consciousness." From these two facts a perfectly logical conclusion is that "Life," "awareness," and even "consciousness" are inherent properties of the Universe. The big difference from what I am saying here compared with what mainstream science implies is <u>the Universe Itself is therefore, alive, aware, and cosmically conscious.</u> The big difference between this viewpoint and what mainstream religion states is <u>the spiritual system of which we are a part is also expanding exponentially</u> (just like the physical Universe). All of us are, therefore, not just alive, aware, and conscious (*in varying degrees*) on this spinning blue planet, but are also vital components within the spiritual expansion of the whole system.

The proofs of this are the signs and signals, which amazingly arrive showing you The Way. This spiritual system appears to "want" you to move from a boring, unfulfilling experience to one of more vibrant expression. One question you should be asking now is, *"What does an inherently aware and expanding Universe have to do with the power of boredom?"* Well, as you shall soon see, everything!

CHAPTER 7

Boredom and the "God Process"

"The adage 'Know Thyself' presupposes a model of the self that is stationary. For knowing the self at any given time actually changes the self into a new knowing self, which must again be known and thus changed."

JANE ROBERTS

"The Spirit will be true to Itself at every level of expression but it will never be completed. If it were ever to be completed, then we should have to add the assumption of completion... and eternal boredom, and then even God would become tired of himself!"

ERNEST HOLMES

et's say you have applied the ideas and practices that I have talked about here so far. You have felt and recognized a gnawing, restless boredom with some aspect of your life. However, you held fast and did not try alleviating this discomfort through distractions or indulgences. Allowing this feeling of boredom to become a building tension, you simply waited. As you waited you kept the high watch like a hawk on a cliff, relentlessly maintaining an elevated level of consciousness. Then being a hunter, you watched carefully for signs and signals indicating the most efficient path toward your greater good. Over time those signs and coincidences came, which you did not ignore or explain away. By carefully, religiously, following these signals you eventually found yourself and your particular circumstances shifted into more interesting, stimulating life situations. In short, you found yourself expressing more Life. The boredom you previously experienced with that aspect of your life you sought to change became a thing of the past. After experiencing your life being transformed through this process time and again, you may have come up with a couple of important questions such as: *"What's this all about?" "Why would the Universe care about me having a richer, more fulfilled life?"*

These very questions haunted me for years as I experienced countless amazing outcomes from this form of Tao-hunting. Out of desperation I slowly learned to quit wasting my precious power. By alert waiting I eventually saw and followed the signs Spirit provided pointing The Way out of boredom into more fulfilling arenas of activity. Quite simply, I was astounded!

One of the most powerful sayings I remember from Bible school days was the one challenging us to *"Knock, Seek, Ask!"* I now see that these three words pretty much encapsulate my lifelong quest for understanding. What I eventually saw, after decades of knocking, seeking, and relentless asking, was the sobering realization that what I am calling, 'The Power of Boredom,' <u>was literally the force behind the expanding Universe.</u> To put this a different way, what I realized was that the Great Spirit of Life was a hunter and stalker as well, and the wild 'game' this Spirit hunts is <u>AWARENESS</u>!

As I mentioned in the beginning of this book, years ago I reached a breaking point while trying to align my scientific knowledge and early religious programming with personal mystical experiences. As I reflected beyond the simplistic explanations of religion, or the mechanistic conclusions of science, a realization slowly dawned that permanently rocked my worldview. I eventually saw our deeply ingrained cultural belief of an "all-knowing God" simply did not work. The story was much larger than this pat, unquestioned belief. With this insight, the puzzle pieces of "Life" slowly began to fall into place and I obtained a glimmer of understanding of what 'IT' (my term for this "God Process") was really all about.

I now need to back up here for a moment to make sure you grasp the importance of what was just said and emphasize its ramifications.

How can anyone state with total confidence that "God" does or does not know all things? Both claims are absurd and obviously impossible for any mortal to prove one way or another. In fact, this question ranks right up there with attempts in estimating how many angels would fit on the head of a pin! What struck me with this realization was how assuming an "all-knowing God" leads quickly to a dead end with respect to the philosophical question on life's meaning. Conversely, the view of a Great Spirit who is exponentially expanding in knowledge is explosive with possibilities. From this viewpoint the long-sought question on life's meaning, both personal and universal, becomes crystal clear.

Let's probe a little deeper into these two philosophical perspectives. Now, try to imagine if you were totally omniscient, that you knew all things. This means you knew everything that would ever happen throughout all the countless worlds in the Universe as well as the outcome of every probability which could ever be expressed. No doubt this would be one heck of a powerful feeling, but then what? From this point there could be no growth or learning because you already knew it all! I realized the state of omniscience would be one of total stagnation and <u>absolutely boring</u> for any intelligent being, even a "supreme" one. From everything I have witnessed and learned about Life on this beautiful blue planet, it is anything but stagnant. Life is an upwelling, an extravagant exploration of potential on a scale that simply cannot be comprehended. Please note here when I say, "Life," I mean this erupting, evolving, beautiful flowering of *aware energy* expressing Itself in countless forms, and <u>NOT just human life</u>.

I'm afraid the possibility is rather high that what I am saying here could be wildly misunderstood. Please realize, therefore, even though I am basically saying that I believe an Omniscient God cannot exist, I am NOT saying there is no Great Universal Being permeating all of existence, including us. The existence of this Omnipresent, supremely intelligent, Spirit is as blindingly obvious as the sun to me now (although it took me some time to get here). This living, growing Great Spirit appears to be totally aware, receptive, and very willing to communicate to those who are open. However, as I will soon explain, this Being simply cannot know all things because if It did, the game would be over. There would be no point! However, in order to grasp this realization you must drop all preconditioning you have of viewing creation, Life, Truth, and even "God" in traditional, simplistic, human terms. This thing called "God," Spirit, the Universe, or, as I prefer, Life is much too big and evocative for that!

Let's now look more closely at this thing called "Life." I will show you how "The Power of Boredom" is the motivating force behind, not just Life, but also this *eternally unfolding* (using Buddha's Lotus metaphor) "God Process."

One of the key realizations allowing Charles Darwin and Alfred Wallace to eventually formulate the world-shattering theory of evolution was the unrelenting pressure of Life to make more individuals or, if you will, "containers." (*I personally like the term 'containers' as it alludes to the surging, overflowing, and relentless flow of Life-force seeking expression through infinite forms.*) It's a simple mental exercise in logarithmic mathematics to see we would be neck-deep in spiders and other bugs in a very short time if their reproduction were allowed to run unchecked. Of course the microbial world, with new generations of bacteria occurring in minutes, would bury us even more rapidly. The point I want you to understand here is how <u>there exists an intense pressure of Life to express Itself any way It can</u>. This is a fact. Both Darwin and Wallace realized this fact as being crucial in understanding how any environmental selection process, such as a change in climate, over time directs this relentless pressure of Life into new, better adaptive forms. After enough accumulated change within these life-forms occurs, we call them "species."

As a young biologist studying about Life in detail, I was staggered by the incredible variety of living things present on this planet (over 350,000 species of beetles alone)! Then, when I realized this amazing variety was only a microscopic thin slice in comparison to all the life forms which were now extinct, my view of our brief human planetary occupancy was permanently shifted. I saw we truly are but a tiny drop in this ocean of Life within the immensity of evolutionary time. For example, science knows now that single-cell bacteria ruled the earth for over <u>three billion years</u> before these cells even learned to work together to construct the simplest of organisms using multicellular strategies! From the fossil record it is clear that even the rise of the mammals, around 60 million years ago, was incredibly recent in the scheme of Life. The tiny Hominid branch of primates of which we belong dates back perhaps only a few million years.

I couldn't shake the troubling questions, *"What's the point of all this?" "Was it all really just a fortuitous accident of chemistry, as the science books and my professors told me?" "Did some random lightning strike in a primordial swamp several billion years ago really initiate life?"* In the scientific community it is accepted as fact, after this "bolt from the blue" inception of Life, that the stepwise advance from organic molecules to Mastodons was just a matter of rolling genetic dice and natural selection choosing the best (or luckiest) players. As a young college student this all sounded very neat and orderly. At the time it was also a big relief to alleviate the need for a capricious, Thor-like God directing circumstances from above. However, something just didn't ring true and the image of Dorothy discovering the "humbug" Wizard, pulling levers behind the curtain in Oz, kept haunting me.

It was impossible for me to keep ignoring what I was experiencing and perceiving. The data gained from my living a hard, fast, and somewhat reckless life simply did not fit this tidy mechanistic model. Inanimate matter did not really seem to be really "inanimate" at times. I noticed more and more that circumstances occurred which were definitely connected in some strange way to my thoughts. Most troubling, I began to get instant agreement to some thoughts by my surroundings such as lyrics on the radio or in the croak of a low-flying raven. Like a young Helen Keller in the movie <u>The Miracle Worker</u>, there seemed to be some sort of communication coming from an unseen world outside time and space, but I didn't quite understand the symbolic language. The obvious question, which eventually emerged due to what I had been experiencing, was: *"What if the Universe truly was a conscious living being?"* Wasn't this exactly what tribes around the world had been saying for a very long time? Maybe these people were not so "primitive" after all.

When I looked closely at the process of Life and Its relentless internal pressure to express Itself, in whatever form selected by the conditions, It appeared to me to be functioning like a vast, probing, amorphous creature. What if the Great Spirit, or what we call "God," was actually <u>LEARNING</u> from the collective awareness of these countless, evolving, probing tentacles of Life? What if this Spirit was actually LEARNING more about Itself, of Its "Being-ness," through all of these individualized expressions, including you and me? What if each of us was a vital, <u>experiential receptor organ</u> on the expanding edge of the possible for this great, growing Being we have called "God?"

There was something about this visualization, this idea that resonated deeply within me. However, the next question was, of course, *"Why go through all the bother if this Spirit, this omniscient "God," already knew everything anyway?"* If you knew the outcome of a billion throws of the dice, every single time, why throw them? Talk about BORING! It was obvious to me that living things, of even moderate intelligence, show an aversion to being bored and will escape any form of captivity given the chance. Why was this? <u>Could this aversion to boredom actually be a quality inherent within the very Spirit of the Universe?</u> Could it be that, "God" is really a "work in progress?" Could the meaning, the purpose behind Life, all of Life, be viewed as an eternal, (and quite impossible) quest to KNOW AND EXPERIENCE ALL THINGS? <u>What if the times of boredom we feel are literally the ache of the Universe, of Buddha's flowering Godhead, to be, to do, and to have more through each of us?</u>

What I have put forth here is a rather large idea as well as a radical departure from what the majority of us were taught to believe from a very young age. Imagine trying to make the point back in Bible school class that perhaps God didn't really know everything yet! This view on boredom gives a completely new philosophical perspective on Life and our soul's purpose in this magnificent Universe. It may, therefore, take some time to wrap your head around what I am saying here and to grasp the profound implications behind all of this. So let me back up and go over the main points concerning the "God Process" one more time.

The most outrageous, mysterious, and inexplicable thing in the Universe is LIFE. Somehow, much to the discomfort of the clockwork scientists, matter became alive, aware, and even conscious of Itself as humans. That a vast intelligence exists behind and within this process has been obvious to mankind's greatest shamans, mystics, and enlightened thinkers throughout the ages. However, there has been endless confusion concerning the purpose behind this rather extravagant enterprise. Because of this confusion there have been countless story lines, mythologies, rationales, and religious fairy tales created giving almost exclusive attention to only human life. Most of these systems depend upon an all-powerful, all-present, all-knowing God, which in our culture seems to be masculine in nature and highly judgmental in behavior. It is my belief, based upon a lifetime of observation, thought, a vision or two, and much feedback from the Universe that all of these systems have mostly missed the point.

Yes, there is a Great Spirit of supreme intelligence, which is omnipresent, and appears to know our thoughts and responds to us in both ordinary and mysterious ways. The critical shift in perspective here is we are not shipwrecked sinners separate from this Being, but actually are IT poured into a fleshy container. This is the perspective supported by all the current New Thought philosophies. <u>Creation is not separate from Spirit but made of It.</u> From this understanding it makes perfect sense that we, as aspects or facets of this Great Being, are really IT learning and expressing through our "living-ness."

What I came to understand was each of our lives, with their unique genetic makeups, embedded within never-before-experienced cultural and environmental circumstances, is a brand new slice of "awareness pie" to this voracious Great Spirit or Cosmic Hunter. The focal point understanding needed for Life (this incessant, erupting biological world) to make any sense is this Being cannot already know all things. Additionally, it is important to understand this eternally hungry Spirit of the Universe is not just feeding upon the awareness of our species, but through the collective experiential awareness of ALL life, even mosquitoes and slime molds! From this perspective it is obvious this great, evolving, growing Being also has as well an unquenchable curiosity. Eternally It is asking the question, *"What if?"*

This morning I watched a sharp-shinned hawk hunt silently through the brush along the river. What's it like to be a hungry hawk on a frosty morning looking for a clumsy sparrow? What's it like being a migrating ruby-throated hummingbird crossing the Gulf of Mexico at night, or a humpback whale singing love songs 700 feet under the Pacific? What's it like to be a peregrine falcon tucked into a 200 mile per hour dive over the Yukon River targeting a clueless duck far below? What is the part of me, and perhaps you, which would love to taste for ourselves each of these deliciously wild experiences? Could this curiosity deep within us be but the smoky wisp of the infinite longing "God" has to know, to experience all things?

An unconscious, agreed-upon attribute our culture has ascribed to the concept of "God" is a Being who knows everything. As I said before, this would be rather boring to any Being of intelligence. Yet what a different perspective is introduced when it is seen that this Being of pure intelligence and profound curiosity has the Divine INTENT to know all things! I believe it is this very INTENT which is the compelling force behind our expanding Universe. Likewise, it is this INTENT that is also behind your longing to expand, to become more as well. This is the motivating power for your desire to move out of boredom and become more. I use the term "God Process" because there can be no end to the expression of this Divine INTENT. There is no end to this eternal expansion of which you are a wonderful, unique, and vital aspect.

Embedded within this "God Process" perspective is an essential principle which must be understood as well. The core reason why there can be no end in this divine quest to know all things is that the expanding "ALL," the Godhead, <u>keeps changing</u>. What I realized was that as Spirit enthusiastically dives into Its creation as the flowing, evolving, energy of Life, every choice, every new combination of variables creates new possibilities, new probabilities. The image that comes to my mind is of a prairie fire running before hurricane-force winds. <u>This "God Process" of attempting to experience all possibilities of Being is the perfect exponential function!</u> Think about this for a moment. The more IT becomes, the more possibilities open up! Isn't it curious that on the physical plane, our expanding Universe is an exact representation of just this?

At first this new view of an expanding, evolving, unfolding "God" might seem strange to you. I am sure some will even take personal offense at a model of a "God" who doesn't know all things. We seem to be living in a time and culture having deep psychological cravings for superheroes to save us from evil forces. It is tough realizing that each of us must eventually be the superhero of our own lives. Any perceived "evil" is really only the result of our individual and collective arrogant ignorance. When we wake up and see our lives have become ones of "quiet desperation," it is up to us to navigate back to our Yellow Brick Road following the signs and signals of Spirit. Those feelings of boredom must not be ignored but <u>seen as the actual aching of the Universe to be more fully expressed through you, in your own unique way.</u> So, do you now understand this power behind your feelings of discontent and boredom is really the very power of the expanding Universe? It is the power of the Great Growing Spirit of Life wanting to be MORE through you! Do you think it wise to ignore such a longing, such a request?

I am sure it sounds like the epitome of arrogance in claiming "God" cannot know all things. How easy it could be for someone reading this to completely miss my point. For us here on the surface of this damp rock orbiting the sun the point is, for the most part, philosophical in nature. Let me explain.

Imagine the gradient in knowledge between you, reading these words, and the knowledge of all the leaders, scientists, healers, and mystics that have ever lived. By comparison, what you personally know and have experienced in your life would be a very small drop indeed. Now, imagine the knowledge gradient between you and an amoeba oozing about in a Texas swamp. To the single-cell amoeba you are a god of truly incomprehensible proportions. Next, try to imagine the knowledge basis of a Being having at its Divine 'finger tips' (so to speak) the collective awareness of every living organism which has ever lived, not just on Earth, but also on every spinning world within our exponentially expanding Universe. Yet, even beyond this, IT also has access to every scrap of awareness from all expanding parallel Universes as well!

From this perspective, the expanding, growing Being we named "God" definitely knows just a bit more than we do. In fact, relative to any individual-ized aspect of this Being It essentially is "all knowing" (just as "you" might seem to any cell of your body). The point I am making here with the concept of the "God Process" is how this incomprehensible Being is anything but static, fixed, or complete. Instead, I propose "God" is really IN THE PROCESS of knowing all things, and each of us are a vital part of this process. <u>We are all evolving root tips of the Great Spirit tree of eternal growth and expansion</u>!

I must admit I found it rather disturbing when these realizations and in-sights were formulating in my mind years ago. This new view of a learning, growing Deity was in very sharp contrast with my Christian upbringing and Catholic education. As you can imagine I kept these realizations to myself. Declaring from the rooftops that our "Heavenly Father" might not actually know all things seemed a fast ticket to a figurative stoning! It was around this time that I discovered the teachings of "Abraham," a collection of non-physical teachers channeled through the amazing Esther Hicks.

What a relief these teachings were! I heard "Abraham" repeatedly commending us during their recordings for being out here on the "ragged, bleeding edge of creation." The whole theme of the Abraham works is for us to recognize we are "co-creators" with "Source Energy" in the process of discovering our unique and evolving preferences through contrasting experiences. They encourage us to follow what they termed "our internal guidance system." By doing so, Abraham states we shall continually grow along the pathways of our wanting, which likewise expands Source. I quickly saw this philosophy being in total agreement with my ideas. In the Abraham philosophy, as with my insights, there is no "getting it done." Expansion on both the individual and Universal (God) level is eternal.

So, to answer the question at the beginning of the chapter, "*what's this all about*" is that this great learning Spirit, this aware, growing infinity, is in essence a hunter, just like you! It is hunting hard through your life, and the lives of all living things, out here on "*the ragged, bleeding edge*" of the possible. This Being can be viewed as feeding upon all experience as IT grows ever more aware by hunting self-knowledge through/as each of us. However, there is a danger here of getting stuck again in the delusion of separation. Ultimately, there can be no "us" and "them" in this eternal system of expansion. As Source expands in self-knowledge, through each experiential probe of Itself, we also become more with even greater possibilities opening before us.

The answer to the nagging old question of "why," is straightforward now. This vast, expanding Being wants us to have an enriched life experience because Its awareness is then enriched and expanded along harmonious probability lines as well.

CHAPTER 8

The Hunger Game

"Blessed are those who hunger and thirst for
righteousness, for they shall be filled."
MATTHEW 5:61

"IT is alive, intelligent, and very hungry."
MEDITATION JOURNAL

Just like the eternally expanding Great Spirit of which it is a part, your soul must ever grow. When it becomes caged, chained, confined within a small living area it becomes restless and hungry for stimulation, for MORE. As I have said, this upwelling spirit-hunger can be felt as so-called "boredom," or perhaps a general dissatisfaction with your life. Like the big cats at the zoo, your soul paces back and forth along the fences hemming in your life, while deep inside, a tension builds. Children demonstrate this the most clearly since they have not yet been fully conditioned to quietly accept their feelings of boredom. They don't want to sit still in the doctor's office waiting room, or on the hard pews in church. They want to go play! After decades of schooling and work, most adults have learned they must keep this wild cat of their hungry soul on a very short leash. We have all learned the hard and unpleasant consequences over the years for not doing this. Yet, the divine spark within us always wants to check out new country, new possibilities. It wants to hunt for MORE!

As mentioned previously, I was very lucky to have learned hunting and stalking skills early in life. From my childhood of hunting small game in the Kentucky woods, on to larger animals of the Rockies and then up in Alaska, my skills sharpened. Try to imagine the state of intense vigilance required when stalking through brushy willow thickets in grizzly bear country! Yet, in time, I found that even this type of hunting pales compared to stalking carefully along the trail of my life following the signs of Spirit! Since awakening to this level of stalking I no longer hunt meat for the table but only for the signs of my magical Way. The reason I am writing this book is for others to discover the joy and excitement of this type of hunting.

However, I realize most of you reading this book have not had the opportunity to learn to hunt as I have. Therefore, I want to describe for you what could be called, "The mindset of the hungry hunter." To be an effective hunter along The Way to a more abundant life, I believe it is vital you develop such a mental attitude. It is only when you are truly hungry for MORE that you become fully engaged in the hunt.

The hungry hunter has pure <u>intention</u>. She knows what she wants and intends to have it. Food! As she slowly moves through the woods and fields, her senses are sharply tuned, yet at the same time, not focused upon any one particular thing. She is on what could be called "scan mode." This includes monitoring her inner senses as well as what's around her because intuition is one of her most important hunting tools. As she slips silently through the brush, pausing often and long, totally in tune with all that is around her, she eventually feels drawn toward a particular clump of bushes near the stream. Moving very slowly, and without even thinking about it, she approaches the area downwind.

(When you are intensely hunting like this there are no thoughts of the future or the past, you are totally in the NOW. This is the NOW Eckhart Tolle so beautifully describes in his books. To be truly effective, you must be as fully present as the game being hunted.)

Through her inner stillness she realizes that she has mindlessly focused upon a small dark spot between the leaves. It seems different in some way. As she waits and watches, the spot blinks and she realizes it is the dark eye of a rabbit! In a very slow fluid motion her bow comes up, and when maximum tension is reached as the string touches her cheek, the arrow is released. Only as she then sees the rabbit's dying kicks, pinned to the ground, do time and her thoughts return. She is filled with relief and gratitude for now she will eat.

Fewer of us in America go hungry these days and not many depend upon their hunting skills for feeding themselves and their families. Of course, this is not true for other places in the world, and certainly not even in our country just a couple generations ago. But hunting is in our blood and all of us come from a long line of successful hunters. Over the tens of thousands of years those individuals and groups who hunted poorly did not survive to pass on offspring. My point is that we all have hunting in our blood even if the thought of killing and eating a rabbit might repulse you. Intense hunger has a way of changing such refined ideas, as numerous individuals lost in the wilderness have discovered.

The type of hunting focused on in this book is not meat for the body but nourishment for the soul. Soul hunger is certainly no less serious than bodily hunger. Perhaps this soul starvation is actually the root cause behind many of the serious problems of our times. Just like a starving body, a starving soul can drive individuals into doing desperate things. How much of the senseless violence, the alcohol and drug abuse, and even the ongoing military insanity around the world are caused by the desperate thrashing of chained, starving souls? Therefore, <u>learning to be attentive to the rustlings of boredom in your life and having the ability to harness the expansive power of your soul seeking MORE, are vital skills for a hunter seeking life-food for the soul.</u>

Yet you might ask, "What is this endless hunger game of the soul all about? What's the point?" The answer to this eternal question comes down really to one word, "*awareness.*" As I explained before, the Universe, Great Spirit, or simply "IT" seeks to expand more fully through you. Period. If you've ever noticed small plants pushing up through asphalt streets, or tree roots busting the city sidewalk, you have had a tiny glimpse of this relentless pressure of Life to expand. I do not believe this process ever really ends or that you will eventually "arrive." We are Spirit hunters of the Way, and that's just what we do; lifetime after lifetime, dimension after dimension. The hunt! The glorious, eternal hunt of GOOD along The Way; this is all that matters to experiential explorers of consciousness!

As you become a more conscious "cooperative component" in this eternal awareness-expansion project, life becomes increasingly mystical and magical. Synchronicities will abound and everyday you will see evidence of a much larger game afoot. However, personal power or spirit-energy is required before this awareness-expansion can really take off. Because you now have quit wasting your precious power when feeling those hunger pangs of boredom, the spirit-energy will rise steadily. This is the true wealth for a resolute hunter of The Way!

I will never forget the ice-water shock I felt upon finally realizing that the Universe truly was "*alive, intelligent, and very hungry.*" This realization is not something which can be handed down, but must be validated anew by each seeker. Although some have become illumined in a single blinding flash, validation for me came slowly by experimenting within the laboratory of my life. Regardless of the process, for all hunters who hunger to realize and experience MORE, <u>awareness is the key</u>.

One way to visualize this kind of awareness is from old film movies. The images on these films were a series of photographs called "frames." The really old silent movies appear jerky because the "frames-per-second" speed was so slow. At the opposite end of this spectrum are the current ultra high-speed movies made now of things like a hummingbird's flight, or even of rifle bullets impacting water balloons. With these films the frames-per-second speed is so rapid that formerly invisible events, such as how a hummingbird's wing works, can be viewed in slow motion. The life-events of individuals having a low-level of awareness can appear jerky just like those old movies. From their vantage point, things just seem to happen to these people with no rhyme or reason. Conversely, if a warrior-hunter, having ample spirit-energy, replaced them within the movie of their life everything would change. Due to their greater "frames-per-second" awareness speed, these hunters would notice the subtle guidance signs/signals and navigate quickly toward better probable event-territory. This is possible due to their increased level of awareness, and as I have emphasized many times, this requires energy.

Because awareness-energy usually takes time to build, many wrong turns will likely be made finding your yellow brick path. In the past I often felt like a drowsy driver trying to navigate through city streets, missing turn after turn. Initially, we are all somewhat asleep in this awareness-hunger-game and frequently veer off course. That's ok as long as we learn the correct way of dealing with these missteps. In short we need to learn how to make mistakes.

CHAPTER 9

How to Make Mistakes

"There are only two (real) mistakes one can make along the road to truth; not going all the way, and not starting."

BUDDHA

"The laws of the universe are there, but we are ignorant of them, and only through experience gained by repeated failures can we get any insight into the laws with which we have to deal."

THOMAS TROWARD

"Mistakes are a bad thing and something to avoid." "People who make many mistakes are usually not too smart and are likewise very unsuccessful." These statements reflect for me our culture's beliefs about making mistakes. We learn this mindset at a tender age in kindergarten when we stray outside the lines coloring or writing. As teenagers, desperate to fit in, we work hard at dressing the right way, talking the right way, and trying to always appear "cool." If you slip up you know how quickly you will be ridiculed. In high school and college our assignments come back all marked up by the teacher's red pen. Later, in the highly competitive adult work world, we are quickly judged if we take a misstep. For the celebrity or public figure who screws up by saying something dumb or inappropriate, the media is very ready to pounce like a pack of hyenas. Of course, religions are filled with strict rules and codes of conduct which, if broken, land you in a heap of trouble. You may be told that you could even end up in Hell on the slow rotisserie grill for, "*like, forever!*"

With this in mind it might sound crazy when I tell you that in this stalking game making mistakes is a good thing. While hunting for your Yellow Brick Road, trying to decipher Spirit's signs, it is important to get out there and not be afraid of making many errors. You have to be willing to take wrong turns and screw up repeatedly. There really is no other way to learn. However, there is a method or approach for making these kinds of mistakes, which will help you to get back on the trail of your good that I will cover shortly. But first I want to outline some mindsets and behaviors that can keep you way off your trail in the sticker bushes for a long time, perhaps even lifetimes! These are the behaviors you need to avoid.

The easiest way to stay lost is to be underlined attached. By this I mean that you feel that you must have things a certain way before even considering any change in lifestyle. For example, let's say you would really like to find a way out of your boring life as long as the path still includes you being able to go out with your high-school buddies and party hard every so often. Perhaps you are attached to staying in the same town where you grew up and close to your family. Your Yellow Brick Road may indeed be there but you just can't be attached to this. The object of your attachment does not really matter; what matters is the blinders you have on limiting your vision of what's possible.

Attachments can take on many forms and be quite subtle. Let's say you think you have gotten a signal or sign that you should drive across town to visit your sick Aunt Sally. That would be sweet, and it makes you feel good to do this. Halfway there, you pick up a signal you should stop at the Barnes and

Noble bookstore. An author you were told about only yesterday just came on your radio for an interview. Traffic is bogged down behind a school bus up ahead, and you are in the right lane to zip into the bookstore. If you are attached to your original plan and talk yourself out of stopping, in this case you will miss a very important connection. While looking for that author's book in the store, your old high-school sweetheart will see you and the rest, as they say, is history.

"Hold on there," you might be saying. "What if Aunt Sally dies while you are chatting with your old flame?" Of course, many other possibilities can be imagined in this rather simple example. My point is to show the importance of being detached from outcomes while on the trail to your good. What I didn't touch upon was what you <u>felt</u> at the moment. With this type of navigating, <u>feelings and hunches can be very important</u>. If I were going to see Aunt Sally, and I felt tightness in my stomach as I considered taking the detour into the store, I would instantly forget the idea and head straight to see my Aunt. The point is that a good hunter must remain alert, open, and flexible.

It has been my experience on this hunter's path that sometimes it has seemed that Spirit was throwing me curves like this every so often, perhaps checking if I was paying attention or becoming fixated on outcomes. If you stop and think about it, ultimately you cannot even be attached to your physical body! Eventually you will have to give it up as well. There is only one thing that you can "legally" be attached to in this power-stalking game. Like a coon-dog on the trail, as a hunter you can only be attached to following The Way, no matter what. You certainly can't be attached to always making the right moves and never making mistakes along this twisting trail!

There is a special flavor of attachment that has been my nemesis and perhaps will be yours as well. This is being attached to "logic." The rational mind is strong in many of us and can put up one heck of a fight to remain in control. It can become the sole filter (soul filter!) through which all decisions must pass before any action is taken or even considered. An offshoot of this mindset is when all decisions are weighed based upon economics. I know people who make every decision concerning what they do, where they go, even when they go, based upon financial cost. This is a special kind of madness that is very common and even somewhat praised in our times. Finding your Yellow Brick Road must take total priority. Sometimes what you feel you should do as you follow Spirit's scent will seem totally illogical to others and perhaps even to you. It may even appear to be fiscally irresponsible. You simply must be willing, from time to time, little by little, to give up your attachment to human logic. This does not mean becoming completely irrational, just relax the death grip of this attachment. Logic is a useful tool in your box, but not the only one.

The cold truth is we simply don't have the vision or computing power to logically evaluate the overall effect of our actions, or inactions. A metaphor which has helped me understand this truth is that of the aerial perspective compared with a surface one.

When living in Alaska I would sometimes take my small airplane up in winter to scout for good places to find dry firewood. The topography of the country was highly convoluted with lakes, marshes, sloughs, and strips of dense willows. From a snowmobile on the surface, it would be a nightmare trying to find a route to a group of dead spruce trees. *(Those of you who may have dealt with 600 pounds of stuck snowmobile know what I mean!)* However, from the air I would map out the best way to connect the frozen lakes and marshes to get to the trees once back on the ground. Later, working out the path I saw while flying, my trail could appear crazy to anyone following. Pulling my wood-hauling sled I would have to zig and zag back and forth, *(sometimes even going in the opposite direction of where I intended to go)* in order to work my way around the many obstacles.

Now, applying this metaphor to following our Power-trail, Spirit has a higher perspective just as I did in the airplane. It can evaluate direction and outcomes through the tangled maze of time and circumstance much better than we can from our surface perspective. To anyone else, the trail you make by following your guidance might appear crazy and irrational as my snowmobile trail appeared on the ground.

As you can imagine, there is plenty of room for error in this process of learning to perceive signs, listening to your intuition, and following Spirit's guidance out of boredom's grip. For me the perfect analogy for this process is imagining young Helen Keller's struggle to make the connection of the unperceived world around her through the finger signs that her teacher, Ann Sullivan, pushed into her hand. Imagine her confusion and imagine all her mistakes! (*I strongly recommend that you watch the old black and white movie version of* The Miracle Worker *to burn this metaphor deep into your brain.*) In this process of spiritual awakening you are learning to deal with a whole new way of perceiving and communicating. It is only through trial and error that you will learn to "see" in this new way. The important thing is being able to progressively learn from your errors and thus refine your intuitive navigation abilities for staying on course.

This brings me to the point where I will explain the all-important technique of how to make mistakes *effectively*. In reality this is a tried-and-true method that has been used with great success for solving all sorts of technical problems for centuries. It is called the scientific method. The twist on this technique here is in applying the steps in a highly personal manner that I refer to as doing "Self Science." Here you mentally apply the steps of the scientific method in order to prove to yourself that the Universe is guiding you along The Way. Before I jump into the steps involved here I want to explain my reasons for using this technique.

Let's face it, this whole philosophy of an aware, responsive, Universe guiding you from boredom with signs and signals goes against what most have been taught to believe. It was very difficult for me to accept and, as I've said, I struggled for many years trying to fit round observations into square-holed beliefs. It is my intent here to save you some of this time and struggle so that you can be on your Way in the happy hunting grounds of your life. When I eventually quit being so self-judgmental and just objectively applied these "self science" steps to events, I began to see the game more clearly. Let's now look at these steps.

In the scientific method you first have a question, then you come up with a hypothesis (or best guess) concerning the answer. Next you come up with some way to test this hypothesis, collect and analyze the data, and then conclude if your hypothesis was correct. In my technique of "Self Science," you follow these same steps to prove or disprove <u>for yourself</u> if these hunches, intuitions, signs and signals are valid or just wishful thinking. A critical component here, just as with "real" scientific studies, is sharp observation skills. You have to be highly alert to notice things like what you are currently thinking and the message on the billboard you just drove past, or the lyrics of the song playing on a store's overhead radio speakers. The big problem with trying to apply the scientific process to intuitive navigation is that it is all so individually unique and highly personal. This is why I call it "Self Science," because you can only do it to yourself as your life events unfold. There really can't be the type of "peer review" which takes place in the scientific community. Here you are strictly on your own. I will talk more about this problem shortly, but for now let's just go over the process and why it is so important.

For example, let's say you have come to realize you need to make a serious change to your life. Your unspoken question in the process will likely be, *"Is there really something better out there waiting for me?"* Perhaps you are rather desperate at this point, (as I was) and decide to try tapping into this power of boredom using the steps I have outlined. Really, what do you have to lose? So your "hypothesis statement" here would be: *<u>"There is a Way out of this situation into a more fulfilling one, and the Universe will guide me to it.</u>"* Because you sincerely intend to find your Way, you cut back on all your power-wasting habits and you begin watching closely for any signs and signals. Since your feelings of life-boredom have not gone anywhere, the tension continues to increase like a bowstring. You want to DO SOMETHING!

It just so happens there is going to be a keg party down at the lake with old friends this coming Friday. You remember how wild these parties can get and you don't want to make a mistake with the stalking of your power. The last thing you want to do is waste your slowly-building spirit energy. Yet, you really want to go and cut loose. Something in your "gut" feels this is probably the wrong thing to do but, "dang it," you really want to go. You decided you're going to the party but mentally you note that you did have some intuitive feelings against it.

On the way to the party there is road construction and when taking the detour you end up with a flat tire. All the while changing the tire you hear mental alarm bells going off, but you choose to ignore them and continue on your way. At this point you are really attached to going. Once at the gathering by the lake things indeed go poorly. After doing some drinking, you get into a fight with the guy dating your old girlfriend. Just as you decide to take your black eye and go home, some loser backs into the side of your truck! The next day, with a pounding headache, you feel drained and stupid. You realize that you intuitively knew better and that you actually ignored the obvious sign of a flat tire. It is at this point you can either continue to beat up on yourself or you can mentally take out your Self Science notebook and record these very good results. With this event you actually gained some excellent data from the experience. You felt you shouldn't go; therefore your intuition was correct. Also, you received a really obvious sign with the flat tire and the chain of negative events. The Universe was talking to you! <u>This is the important thing</u>.

By looking upon your navigational mistakes as if you were testing a scientific hypothesis, you will gain valuable data, even if the data is negative. As your commitment to the stalking process increases and your attachments decrease, you will eventually follow some possible signals, perhaps even against what you want to do, and discover later that the intuition or signs were totally correct.

Just recently I was tested on a camping trip in the desert country of eastern Oregon. Late in the day I began to consider where I was going to park my truck camper for the night. After looking at the map, I decided I wanted to drive back a long gravel road up into the mountains. When I reached the intersection of this road I noticed there was a small public campground down by the creek. Even though I wanted to get going up the mountain road, I got a feeling that I should check out the campground. I pulled into a campsite and sat in my truck feeling things out. Something felt good here, yet I hardly ever camp in campgrounds. First, you have to give them money (logic!) and then there are always noisy neighbors with dogs, etc. *"Nope, I want to go up the mountain."* As I pulled away I got a solid signal/sign I should stay here. Another truck pulled up to read directions at the entrance had blocked my way out. Quickly factoring in my intuitive feelings and the obvious sign, I released my attachment to solitude up the mountain road. I turned my truck around and pulled back into the campsite by the stream.

The sun was setting as I started to place my boards down under the tires to level the truck. As I was bent over the rear tire I heard a hissing sound! Yep, my tire was going flat and here I was in a perfect setting. The truck was on flat, grassy ground, with just enough daylight to change it out. Later on that night I actually did end up hearing some dogs barking, but that was OK. I caught the signals and was at the right place. Such events might seem rather trivial, but they are very important in learning to trust and follow your "gut," or intuition. You are literally <u>learning to follow the Universe's sign language just like Helen Keller had to learn the sign language from her teacher</u>. This takes constant practice.

Therefore, the way to make use of possible mistakes is to<u> be very mindful of pre-event hunches and post-event results.</u> Mentally keep track of them and never write anything off as being "just a coincidence." For me personally, it has been a painfully slow process involving decades. Being just a tad headstrong, I tend to go off in the opposite direction of instructions. Because of this rebel mindset, I made many, many stupid mistakes before becoming *"willing to learn."* The real turnaround for me came when I had to admit how much better life seemed to go when I just followed my hunches and signs, even when at times they pointed in direct opposition to what I wanted or <u>logically</u> thought best. <u>It just became obvious that my little brain didn't have the computational power to juggle all the variables and foresee the best long-term outcomes within the swirling cloud of probabilities.</u>

By following this process of "Self Science" and making mistakes "correctly," you build faith. This is not the "blind faith" so frequently endorsed in religious circles. Instead, this is a<u> scientific faith</u> that you personally have painstakingly built over time through experience. There is nothing "blind" about it. It is faith in the power of the expanding Universe motivating you toward a richer, more abundant life. This faith is not a "hand-me-down faith." It did not come from some organized group of believers based only upon what they have been taught. This is the faith of the hunter who has learned to read and follow sign.

While practicing this "Self Science" you should naturally keep the process to yourself. You are developing a communication system between you and the Universe. It is a private conversation. Talking about it, trying to explain why you decided to go this way or not do that, just opens you up for ridicule and reduces the Spirit power you are trying to build. Eventually, down that Yellow Brick Road, you may find a few special individuals who understand this process as well and will support you.

As I indicated earlier there are problems with not having a means of "peer review" when engaged in the "Self Science" process. Even in the prestigious ivory towers of Science there have been many cases of scientists fudging their data to get the results they predicted or wanted. When engaged in this process of following your intuition and reading signs, the possibilities for self-deception are endless. It is essential that you maintain a degree of healthy skepticism and some analytical detachment so that your decisions are not excessively influenced by what you want to see or have happen. <u>This is hard.</u> The image that comes to mind is that of constantly walking a razor's edge. On one side is the world of the hardened materialistic skeptic, where all spirituality is 'hogwash.' On the other side is the nebulous world of superstition, evil forces battling angels, where all scientific rationality is worthless. The key, as in so many things, is maintaining a balance.

Back when I was in chemistry classes we often used analytical balances to weigh out our chemical reactants and products during labs. The first step was always to make sure the scale was "zeroed out" where one side was perfectly balanced by the other side. I would then put the chemical I wanted to weigh on the one side and next, using a series of standardized brass weights, determine how many grams I had. In doing our process of "Self Science" one must attempt to remain as neutral as a zeroed-out scale. Only with this mindset can you at times detect the very light touch of Spirit on the other side nudging you. If you are leaning hard on one side of the scale because of your attachments or fears, you will have a hard time detecting any subtle guidance from the Universe. <u>The true work that never ends is trying to keep that zero balance on your scale in order to better detect the often-delicate touch of Spirit.</u> *(I should mention here that it has been my experience during times when I am being exceptionally dull, missing important turns, that Spirit's touch has been more like that of a crowbar along the side of my head!)*

Finally, I must address the danger that someone could possibly take what I am saying here and twist it into license to cause all sorts of mischief and mayhem. We have all before heard of cases where some badly unbalanced individual does something stupid or terrible and then says that, *"The voices told them to."* Your path, your personal Yellow Brick Road, will always be life-enhancing and never violent or personally destructive. You must forever be on guard to assure that the guidance you are receiving is coming from higher vibrational realms. Keeping your own vibration or Level of Consciousness at a high level assures this. Affirmations, meditation, and inspirational studies will all serve to keep you up to the level where a hunter of Spirit Power needs to be.

The real danger with mistakes is the potential for self-judgment and self-incrimination. You have to keep trying, keep taking chances, and keep getting back up to learn from your errors. By judging your mistakes and being hard on yourself, you are actually lowering your Level of Consciousness, and thus your sensitivity for receiving spiritual guidance. The goal, which may be difficult to imagine when starting out on this journey out of boredom, is to maintain an attitude of amused curiosity as you move carefully along your Yellow Brick Road into a more joy-filled life. Yet, because we are stuck down here in the flatlands of linear time, our vision is severely limited. We can easily get off track in the tangles and backwaters of our lives. However, the Great, growing Spirit of the expanding Universe always sees possible pathways for us toward a richer, more fulfilling life experience. Finding and following this pathway, this personal Yellow Brick Road, is our challenge and the only worthwhile mission in life. So now let's look more closely on how to do this.

CHAPTER 10

Finding the Yellow Brick Road

*"For me there is only the traveling on paths that have heart...
There I travel, and the only worthwhile challenge is to traverse
its full length. And there I travel looking, looking, breathlessly."*

DON JUAN MATUS

"Toto, I don't think we're in Kansas anymore."

DOROTHY

So there you are. In a job, a relationship, or a life situation driving you nuts and boring you to tears. The problem many of us have is we might not even realize it; we have become "comfortably numb." You could even be rich and successful in the eyes of the world; this doesn't matter if you're off the Yellow Brick Road. Money and fame are not really important to your soul. It is totally possible, even after making all the right moves, (according to "the world") to end up in a successful dull life. Boredom has no favorites and like rain "falls upon the just and unjust alike." You might decide it's better to merely shove your soul's yearnings under the rug and just keep trudging along the comfortably boring road of your life. *"Forget these crazy ideas and see instead if there's something good on TV. What's the worst that could happen anyway?"*

OK, here it comes, hard, fast, and right across the plate: The worst that could happen is you will grow old and die unfulfilled, unexpressed, and very unhappy. I don't think, personally, there is much worse than going down this road! This possibility alone should be enough to motivate you to listen more closely to boredom's whisperings (or screams) and then desperately seek your way back onto your personal Yellow Brick Road. The good news, the wonderful news, the outrageous news is the very <u>Intent of the expanding Universe is totally behind you doing just this</u>! All you have to do is align yourself with this Intent and hang on. Just realize there could first be a period of waiting before your Spirit-power tide rises, floating you off the mudflats you wandered out on.

The best analogy I have for this time of waiting is of a reservoir slowly filling behind a hydroelectric dam. In this analogy the water represents our spiritual energy. In our thrashing about in the brush and muck, wasting our power with endless distractions, it is as if we have left the dam gates opened wide for years and years. The water level in the lake, our precious spiritual energy, has dropped lower and lower. During the exuberance of youth we do not realize the flowing water from our Spirit Lake is what gave the very energy for our lives by turning the dam's turbines. As the lake's level drops over time, the generator's turbines turn ever more slowly. Suddenly, we are shocked to discover how little Life-energy is now available to use. Heavy with the years of worry and responsibility, we are now easily exhausted. It can seem our luck has left us high and dry. So we plod through our remaining days finding solace only on the couch or in a recliner during evenings holding a TV remote firmly in hand.

While we were young and frisky, the amount of Spirit energy appeared almost endless. We didn't walk, we either ran or skipped and each day was an adventure. Perhaps you know, as I do, some rare adults who have been able to maintain this exuberance of youth. They seem to instinctively know the importance of conserving their precious power. Spirit waters from the mountains continue to flow strongly into them. This flow keeps their lakes deep and their energy levels high. However, for many of us it seems we have almost flushed our precious spiritual waters out by the time we reach middle age. It also appears that all are not born having the same size reservoirs. Some people are able to waste more energy for longer than others. Regardless, the cold reality is each of us has but a limited supply of this precious "juice."

When the realization comes in our lives that we are way off our path and literally out of juice, our only hope is to shut down the many opened energy gates wasting our precious power. It is here where most people fail. They desperately try to hang on to their youth through an endless variety of energy-depleting indulgences or activities. This, of course, only makes matters worse and the prisons, hospitals, and graveyards are overflowing with the end results. It is NOW when we must change our energy-depleting ways and patiently wait upon the waters from on high to refill our reservoirs.

If you are like me this waiting will not be fun. However, it is much easier to do when you understand WHY YOU ARE WAITING. For some it may even appear there is a divine conspiracy of some sort in play. What I mean here is a flow of circumstances shuts you down and makes you wait. Some may end up in prison, as in the case of Nelson Mandela, some become desperately ill, or even involved in an accident where all they can do now is wait for Spirit's rain. Historically, there are numerous examples of individuals who were forced to wait for long periods of time and afterwards went on to change the world, no doubt using the Spirit power stored through a waiting process. I speculate this may have even been the case for Jesus, undoubtedly the most influential person in history.

In addition to merely waiting you can also increase the flow of Spirit's waters by developing a stronger, more open connection to what's been aptly called "Source." For me this involves spending hunks of time alone in wild areas submersed in Nature and meditation. For others it may be art, floating rivers, or spending time with children, animals, or even plants. If we become quiet and listen, intuitively we will know those activities that fill us up and those depleting us. No matter what, and this is important to remember, there will usually be some waiting involved. This waiting can be thought of as a test of Intent for finding your personal Yellow Brick Road in life. During such times it is imperative to remain alert for any synchronous patterns of events, books, dreams, and even thoughts. Such patterns often can be quietly providing clues as to the direction you should be moving.

A few chapters ago I said it is the Universe's Intent to express Itself along harmonious, resonant pathways I referred to as "The Way," or the "Tao." Even a superficial study of nature reveals patterns upon patterns of symmetry, from the arrangement of developing sunflower seeds to the spiral curves within the cochlea of your ear. There is something which resonates within us to this natural symmetry and calls it "beautiful." <u>Natural, beautiful patterns of symmetry are possible as well within the events of your life if you allow them to unfold.</u> This is what your personal Yellow Brick Road is all about.

You probably know individuals whose lives reflect this natural flow and they radiate grace and beauty in whatever they do. Likewise, you might also know individuals whose lives reflect the gracelessness of a bulldozer plowing ahead through life totally self-absorbed. When you make the decision of finding your harmonious path of heart, your Tao path, and become totally committed to the process, the awesome power of the expanding Universe will be right there waiting. This unlimited power is what your feelings of boredom will lead you to, if you only allow.

Oh, I can hear in my mind the groans and moans and possibly even references to "bovine manure." I know. I would have totally agreed with you some years ago. It took me decades of blundering around, running into walls while running out of energy, before I began to see and trust the signs and signals pointing me along my Way. It is possible that we all must go through these periods of darkness before seeking the Light. There is a saying I remember picking up from somewhere along the journey: *"Only after you have suffered enough, will you be willing to learn and change."* Unfortunately, this seems too often the case.

I just want to assure you that once you make this connection with the Universe, and experience the thrill of actually recognizing and following your trail of signs, your life will never be the same. You will have become a hunter of The Way! Yes, it is likely you will have to make some scary changes in the process. Eventually, however, you notice your life situation has indeed improved. As you become more confident in your ability to recognize Spirit's signals and more courageous in following the twists and turns of The Way, you might eventually find yourself in a whole new country, much like Dorothy when she landed in Oz. From the dreary, mundane black-and-white world, you now awaken into a colorful, magical place. Although others will probably ridicule you and poke fun at these crazy ideas if you tell them, you now have no intention of going back to the cold, fearful world of the "sensible skeptic." With your ruby slippers snuggly on your feet, you can now go skipping off toward Oz, maybe even with some strange friends you met along The Way.

Before you travel very far down this road, however, you will come face to face with many intersections. Another term for these alternate pathways is "probabilities," and the ability to navigate through these intersections is the true skill and art of hunters stalking power along their Way.

CHAPTER 11

Pool Hall Probabilities

"It was a screaming nightmare. The chimps were all over the pool tables, throwing balls, crapping in the pockets, smacking each other with cue sticks, eating the chalk. Over in the corner of that smoke-filled room of chaos, a fat man sat watching with icy blue eyes. In a disgusted sigh he let out a cloud of blue smoke from his spent cigarette and deftly bent over his table quickly breaking the triangle of balls poised at the far end. At the sharp crack of the break the room went silent and all chimp eyes followed Jackie Gleason[†] as he then systematically cleaned the table calling each and every shot."

2003, DREAM JOURNAL ENTRY

t is through conserving the rising power beneath your boredom and faith-fully following the signs and signals through life's probability maze that you will be led to new, exciting possibilities. Therefore, as a hunter of The Way it is essential that you have a clear understanding of probabilities. It is these wandering threads, through time and events along the trail of your expanding good, that you actually are stalking. Let me clarify what I mean by the term, "life's probability maze" using another childhood memory.

---

† Many of you may not know who "Jackie Gleason" was or know the story (or movie) of "Minnesota Fats." You may want to check out some of the great video clips on Mr. Gleason from this old movie online.

When I was around ten years old I learned how to shoot pool during vacations our family took by the shores of Lake Erie. My younger sister and I would hang out at a little Army base canteen on the beach while my father competed in the National Rifle matches taking place there at Camp Perry. The beach canteen was mostly deserted in the mornings and the two of us had a blast slamming those pool balls around the table. The whole game was wonderfully new to me. My favorite part was doing the break and some balls usually ended up flying off the table rolling all over the room. I was a very enthusiastic pool player! After several summers I even became fairly good at the game but never got really serious about it. Over three decades later, in my struggles to find my path, I came to appreciate and understand on a deeper level those early lessons from the pool hall. In short, I began thinking very hard about probabilities.

As you hunt for signs of your Yellow Brick Road you need to be very mindful of probabilities. It is vital to sense the tangled multitude of threads branching out from each of your decisions and actions. These timeline threads need to be navigated correctly if you are to efficiently move from your place of boredom, or dissatisfaction, to the pathway of your "good and plenty" calling to your soul. Everyone can look back on their lives identifying critical intersections where something someone said, or a seemingly minor decision at the time, led to major life changes. Whenever there has been a big disaster, such as the sinking of the Titanic or the collapse of the World Trade Center, there are always those few individuals who managed to avoid being present due to a gut feeling or some seemingly insignificant chain of circumstances. As you follow the signs and signals along your path toward a more abundant life, try to constantly visualize the divergent probability tracks taking off from each decision. If you are detached and connected with Spirit, you will usually have some sense or feeling of the best way to go. More often than not, the signs, feelings and course corrections will be vague and not very clear. I found this especially so when I was just learning this type of temporal-navigation stalking. Now is the time to move cautiously, alert for any signs of resistance. (*You should also be alert for signs of "joy" which I will discuss later in the book.*)

To me, one of the most tragic events of our generation, prior to the World Trade Center disaster, was the explosion of the space shuttle Challenger on takeoff in 1986. The crew lost was made up of some of the finest individuals our country had to offer, including the exuberant, outstanding teacher, Christa McAuliffe. The signs not to launch on that record cold Florida morning were overwhelming. Warnings from engineers about possible O-ring fuel-seal leaks due to the cold were ignored. If I remember correctly, the crew even had difficulty entering the shuttle due to an iced up frozen door! Yet the momentum of the rational minds in charge was such that they were completely oblivious to the alarm signals due to "go fever." To be fair, they were under tremendous pressure from all corners, but it was not long before those in charge tasted the bitter cost of their arrogant mistake.

When you are carefully moving through probability threads, feeling your way back to your path, be alert for signs of resistance. Perhaps things just seem to be getting more and more difficult or are plainly going wrong. I am certainly not saying that when stalking through the woods of your life you should stop and run away if you meet any resistance. Just be mindful of it. Perhaps the message is merely for a minor course correction, or maybe you are simply missing something important in your eagerness to move (*my chronic issue*). Merely realize, even if you are all dressed in white and everyone is in church waiting for you to walk down the aisle, that you must always be ready and willing to cancel the mission. <u>Spirit must always come first.</u> Yes, it is possible you could have misread the signs and then overreacted. (*Been there, done that!*) Mistakes will be made, but you must be willing to make these mistakes for the right reason. This reason is trying to follow The Way instead of following your ego or reacting to the opinions of others. Later, down the road, you might discover what you previously thought was a mistake was really the ideal shot.

A very important message concerning probabilities came to me from my childhood memories of shooting pool. Every time you strike one or more balls on the pool table the whole game changes. Back in those pool hall days on the shores of Lake Erie, these changes were usually totally random. But for talented pool players, such as Mr. Gleason of my dream, they certainly are not. Very much like a game of chess, a "pool shark" is able to mentally see how each precise cue ball impact will set up subsequent shots in the future. Master pool players can literally run every ball on the table right from the break, calling the pocket of each shot. They have the ability to see all the possibilities laid out before them and then perfectly line up the next shot from the rebounding energy of the previous one. <u>A master hunter of The Way unconsciously does the same thing with probabilities through waiting, listening, and following.</u>

The people, situations, and events of our lives can be viewed as pool balls scattered upon the table of time. It appears to me that the game of most people's lives is played more like bumper cars in an amusement park than pool. There's apparently little thought given to the ramifications and downstream interactions of their colliding actions. For them life is all just "pedal to the metal," hoping for the best, as they bounce off one event into another in a mindless probability chain reaction. I can certainly relate to this method of living since this is exactly how I navigated through much of my life. However, some individuals have the opposite problem due to their fear of acting and this also affects the probability trails expressed by their lives. Because of these ways of living (mindless or fearful) we end up in tangled, boring, and possibly desperate life situations. Navigating your way back upon your Yellow Brick Road is all about learning to become more like a pool-shooting master when it comes to dealing with the constantly changing probabilities we encounter along our green velvet table of time.

Down here at eye level, with the bouncing, rebounding "event balls," the problem we all face is our limited vantage point. Unlike the pool shark, here on the table of time we are simply unable to see the lay of all the balls. In a sense, we are like blind pool players. Now, however, since we are connecting with Spirit and attentive to the inner and outer signs guiding us, this is OK. What we must learn to deeply appreciate is the dynamic nature of this probability maze of our daily lives. Every moment the probability event-balls surrounding us are changing constantly like a bucket of slippery, twisting eels. Timing is everything and there will be times when you must simply SLOW DOWN!

As a metaphor for this, imagine approaching a busy city after taking a leisurely drive in the country. Your life has been chugging along smoothly, and the ride mostly pleasant. Suddenly you notice lanes of traffic merging from both sides along with numerous signs and arrows indicating approaching exits and intersections. While moving along the probability maze of our lives there will be times when you find yourself entering congested probability-thread traffic. Multiple paths will be branching off like interstate highway exits and the possibility of making a wrong turn becomes high. When you intuitively recognize these times, just as you do when driving your car, you need to <u>slow down and watch even more carefully for signs and signals.</u> In your life there will be times such as these when what you do (or don't do) will have strong rippling effects, not only for you, but in the lives of others as well. Unfortunately these times of probability-thread congestion can happen with little warning and you must learn to quickly recognize the flashing yellow caution lights coming toward you.

I am sure you are now wondering, "*What would these 'caution lights' look like?*" It may just be an anxious feeling or a few minor impediments in a row, such as your car doesn't want to start, after it does you see you are out of gas, and your cell phone dies. Note the important thing here can be the overall context of the events, such as all of the events above causing you to be late for a party or important meeting. Or you could eventually develop personal signs as I have with the Universe, like the appearance of certain animals, or even lyrics of a song on the radio. It is really hard to describe such communication because it is so individual. For me it is usually a combination of signs (*even flashing yellow lights!*) and intuitive feelings letting me know an important probability intersection is approaching. By not catching or heeding these warning signs you can blast right through and end up taking the wrong exit, as I have done many, many times.

I know some will quickly scoff at all of this as being just "superstitious mumbo jumbo." Yes, from the outside it can appear so. The critical factor is the level of awareness of the individual noticing these various signs and signals. Over time there comes a level of spiritual discernment giving you an inner "heads up" on noticing a string of apparently random events. This takes time, this takes practice, and this stalking the flow of event-currents definitely takes a different kind of attention.

An important point to keep in mind when dealing with probabilities is what I call "The Exclusion Principle," borrowing from chemistry. When I miss a turn along my way because I was attached, fearful, dense, or suffering from ego intoxication, I always feel it. Perhaps not right away, but later lying in bed that night, or possibly even days after the fact, the image of this particular interaction or decision will resurface along with the uneasy feeling of having "messed up." The resultant probability strand I ended up on is usually not dangerous or "bad" in any way. It may not be a big deal. Yet, I know because I am now upon this particular line of personal reality, I have likely <u>excluded</u> other more resonant, harmonious pathways. Like a sailor of olden days stuck in the doldrums region of the ocean, waiting for a wind to fill my sails, there have been occasions where I have ended up waiting, years sometimes, for Spirit to blow me back on track after missing such turns. Since waiting patiently is a real struggle for my hyperactive nature, these occurrences have taught me to be just a little more cautious while zooming along the probability highways of life.

Recently I took a road trip using a new GPS system my wife bought me as a gift. What an amazing world we live in where such a little device on the dashboard can direct you, after consulting with orbiting satellites, to practically any address. In some ways this system is a good metaphor for finding and following your Yellow Brick Road. Just realize our little technological-miracle of the GPS is but a crude shadow of the sensitive inner guidance system within each of us that I have been discussing. With this understood, you could think of this inner GPS standing for your "Good Path System." Just like the GPS in your car, your inner guidance system will instantly calculate the best route back to your

Yellow Brick Road. When you get sidetracked, start to wander, or miss a turn, a new probability route to your good is calculated without fail. Of course, if you are falling asleep at the wheel, drunk, or just not paying attention to indicated course corrections, you will certainly stay lost!

On a recent road trip I was amused how the woman's voice coming from my GPS on the dashboard never gave up on me when I wandered off course. Instead, she relentlessly informed me of opportunities to either take an alternate route back or good places to turn around. The point I want to emphasize here is no matter how lost we think we are, there exist probability-routes back to our greater good and a system ready, willing, and able to guide us there. However, just as in traffic situations, it may take some time and many twisting turns to return upon your golden probability thread.

As I have said, when you are hunting the power within your boredom, what you are really doing is stalking probabilities. The Yellow Brick Road is simply the golden string of probabilities leading to a more abundant life. Therefore, to be a hunter of The Way, you must be sensitive to the branching probabilities surrounding you each moment. Likewise, you need to be mindful of the resultant spin-offs from your decisions and actions. This takes a special kind of attention few seem to have, and this attention takes ENERGY. This necessary energy increases as you wait patiently, or not so patiently, for the filling of your spirit-power reservoir. Do you understand now why conserving your personal spirit-power is such an important prerequisite to finding your Way? As you regain this precious energy and the subsequent attention required over time, you may now start seeing yourself as a "probability gardener." Being such a gardener, you are now fully committed to life-enhancing probabilities and raising crops of radiating probability threads of good. This is what your Tao truly is: vibrant, growing, and richly productive fields of resonant personal probabilities.

Being a hunter of The Way, always try to envision all the probabilities extending out from your present "now-point" into the future like a spider's web. Each choice, each decision to act or not act will send vibrations through time out into this web of possibilities. The really crazy thing I have found is that this web-work extends not only into the future but also back into what we call the "past" as well. This is why your point of NOW is so important and powerful. From there anything is possible!

CHAPTER 12

The Spider Web of Time

"Even before they call, I will answer; while they are still speaking, I will hear."

ISAIAH 65:24

"A crystal expresses the perfect symmetry of molecular structure. It can be perfect and whole, yet still grow in infinitely beautiful ways. Like a snowflake, like God."

MEDITATION JOURNAL, DEC. 2006

As you are skipping along your golden path you might start to notice something odd as events unfold. It can seem at times that time itself is behaving strangely. We have all been schooled very rigorously about time flowing in a straight line from past to future and how "cause" always precedes "effect" along this line. This learning is almost as deep and unquestioned as our early and sometimes painful lessons concerning gravity when we learned to walk. It is disconcerting to realize our rigid belief about the nature of time needs updating. One problem I've encountered is when "effects" sometimes seem to precede "causes." It becomes difficult to ignore situations where the events necessary for a sign you've received were initiated long before the need for its guidance.

For example, let's say your feelings of boredom have led you to consider quitting your current waitressing job in Denver. It is getting you nowhere and the relationship you have fallen into while living here has become a total energy drain as well. Why not just move back home to Phoenix? You could stay with your sister, help her with her kids, and maybe even attend a local art school. This would be a huge change, but deep down you have wanted to someday get back into art and watercolor painting. Bittersweet memories of how you loved painting as a child have been leaking through recently.

Over the past six months, after reading a crazy book about the power of boredom, you have quit partying, taken to hiking in the hills with your dog, and been watching carefully for "signs." Then yesterday, while mindlessly cleaning your apartment, you happened to come across that shoebox of old letters your mother sent while you were away in college. She passed on some five years ago and you forgot about this box of letters pushed deep in your closet. The sadness of her loss has kept you from wanting to reopen those memories. But now, holding the dusty shoebox in hand, it somehow feels right to open it tonight and you randomly pull a letter from the stack. Out of the envelope a small painting you did for your mother back in high school falls on the floor.

In this letter your mother talks about how proud she is of your artistic abilities, mentions some troubles your older sister is having, and ends with a glowing description of the beautiful winter weather in Phoenix. Your hands are shaking as tears well up in your eyes. As a hunter of the Way you see and understand. The tension on the arrow has been released and you begin to pack your bags.

In the above example the need of the daughter for guidance "now" drew a sign from the "past" within the multidimensional web-work of time. On your mystic-hunter's path, the apparent one-way direction of time, as well as "cause" and "effect," can appear twisted to the rationally programmed mind. Don't worry about it. Just see and follow, always being ready to turn on a dime. Do you remember how the Yellow Brick Road in the Wizard of Oz movie was initially twisted and spiraled?

Some of you may have already seen that there is another larger issue which needs to be discussed concerning time and the "God Process." It may seem I am implying that this expanding, learning, "becoming all that IT can be," Great Spirit of the Universe is doing all of this within linear time. Not so. I see the process more like a growing, multifaceted crystal. The events in our lives do appear to occur in a linear fashion, but the deeper you examine the arrangement of these events, especially once you find and follow your winding Yellow Brick Road, you will see your life as a beautiful, growing crystal. Time is simply one medium in which the crystal of your soul is growing. The purpose behind this soul-crystal growth is to reflect and refract the One Light of Source in totally unique ways. What else would a Being of incalculable energy and intelligence do with eternity?

CHAPTER 13

Boredom, Curiosity, and Joy

"We keep moving forward, opening new doors, and doing new things, because we're curious and curiosity keeps leading us down new paths."
WALT DISNEY

"There cannot be anything true about the individual unless it is first true about the Universe."
ERNEST HOLMES

n the beginning of this book I alluded to an interesting relationship between boredom and curiosity. This relationship is one that is not readily apparent on first glance. These seemingly opposing states are merely ends of an internal magnet potentially moving you toward MORE. When something is boring to me, I tend to retract from it, withdrawing my attention, such as when someone starts telling me his or her life's story at a party. However, if my curiosity is piqued by something, my attention swings like a weather vane in that direction. (*While you are being held captive by that long-winded story, you happen to overhear parts of a whispered conversation concerning a powerful near-death experience from a group be-hind you).*

All higher animals seem to share this faculty of curiosity, just as they do feelings of boredom. Hunters around the world have used this trait for eons to lure game within range. Antelope will come to a waving handkerchief tied to a stick, and I have seen this technique work as well with caribou out on the northern tundra. Beings of intelligence seek to avoid confinement within boring environments and express a built-in curiosity as well. I find this, well, "curious."

When I visualize periods of boredom it seems as if I am facing toward some shadowy, dull time of life and I want to turn away from it. Curiosity, on the other hand, feels as if some sparkle in the periphery caught my eye and I start pivoting away from the shadow side toward that light. For me there is also a feeling of joy linked to mentally being "in the light." What I find intriguing is the similarity in orientation or movement resulting from these opposing mental states. Both act to direct me toward MORE. To me, one appears as an internal "push" away from, and the other a "pull" toward. We tend to push away from experiences that are boring to us and pull toward those that we find curious or interesting. Indeed, they each can function as internal, felt-sense guides indicating course corrections toward a richer, more interesting life experience. Some of you will notice the similarity of this to the "internal guidance system" described in the Abraham-Hicks philosophy. Now, taking this a step further, "Where did these innate states of attraction and repulsion originate?"

Science would have us believe that the ability to feel both boredom and curiosity are simply useful evolutionary adaptations. Perhaps. Yet I believe they go much, much deeper.

In the chapter on the "God process," I proposed that the Spirit of the expanding Universe seeking expression was behind our turning away from boredom. Our intelligence must also be part of Its intelligence and that un-fathomable intelligence simply doesn't like being bored any more than you do! Likewise, doesn't it follow that there must also be a "divine curiosity" expressed by all higher animals? If so, can you see what this implies about, not only the purpose of Life in general, but your life's purpose in particular? <u>You are a prob-ing tentacle tip of an incomprehensible, curious Being ever seeking MORE</u>! The shadowy shape of your boredom and the sparkles of your curiosity both can guide you toward richer, deeper veins of "living-ness."

This is a good point to address the place of "joy" in the process of hunting for your path. *"Is not focusing upon feelings of boredom a negative way to view all of this?"* *"Why not instead just stalk your feelings of joy?"* Absolutely! This method has been succinctly described as, *"following your bliss,"* and it certainly works. The problem I've had with this technique, and you may have as well, is that in comparison to my frequent dark feelings of boredom, flickers of joy or bliss were as rare as hen's teeth. When you're far off the Yellow Brick Road of your life, and your spiritual reservoir is very low in juice, "joy" can be just a three-letter word. It might take some time to build up enough Spirit energy before glimmers of joy begin to sneak back once in awhile. Of course, the most effective strategy to use in finding and following your shining path is to use both your feelings of boredom and joy as guides.

Many years ago, when I was stuck in a very boring job heading nowhere, I was desperate for a change. Driving to work day after day I found my atten-tion being constantly pulled toward bright yellow school buses passing either on the road or at intersections. What I eventually noticed was a delicate soul-flutter, a lightness within, which stirred upon seeing them. It took some time before a flicker of an idea sprouted that, someday, I would like to be a teacher. Of course there was no way I could afford to go back to school to do this! The negative feelings pushing me away from my loser job were the obvious signs coming from my boredom. In contrast, the flickering feelings of lightness (pre-joy) when thinking of being a teacher were pulling me forward toward my MORE. The important thing was that I consciously noticed this. Therefore, I was somewhat prepared for a wild chain of circumstances that soon transpired allowing me to go back to school being retrained as a teacher. What had initially seemed like a "bad" event *(I was injured at my job)* turned out to be a positive kick in the rear from the Universe toward my Way.

To summarize now, both your dark feelings of boredom as well as your light feelings of curiosity and joy can guide you toward your Way. The vital component is you developing a sufficient Level of Consciousness plus enough spiritual energy to notice these guiding influences. The Universe will provide subtle (and sometimes, not so subtle) clues for you to follow toward your "better yet to be." It might take some time, it might take some work, and often it will necessitate big life changes, but know that Spirit has a vested interest in your success! If you stop and think about it, is there really anything more important for YOU to be doing with the limited time you have left? However, before "you" can really understand any of this you must come to terms with a very basic question. *"Just who the heck are you anyway?"*

CHAPTER 14

Who are You?

*"There are three things extremely hard: steel,
a diamond, and to know one's self."*
BENJAMIN FRANKLIN

Several times now I have used the hypothetical example, *"You find that you have become bored or dissatisfied with some aspect of your life."* The critical question not really addressed yet is, *"Who really is this 'you' who is bored?"* This might seem just a bit esoteric, especially if all you want to do is get that "good job" or find that "perfect relationship." However, I assure you, the essence within and behind your desire for more lies in answering this question.

Right now, look at your hand. Wiggle your fingers. Is that hand "you," or are you the energy of the muscles tugging on the tendon cables? What about the computer sending these messages down neural wires? Is that the real you? Who exactly is this "you" who is feeling bored in the first place? The hunger pains of your boredom are certainly real. Like a plant in a small pot, the root tips of your soul are probing for more room and richer soil. But, <u>what is the thing inside you feeling this hunger to expand, and what does this hunger imply</u>?

This brings us to a critical point in our explorations into this strange phenomenon of "boredom." It is sketchy territory with much room for speculation. Yet it has been from my explorations within this wild country of thought that I have uncovered what I believe to be pearls of great value. As I mentioned previously, discovering the meaning of Life in general, and my life in particular, has been a passion from a very early age. In my quest for this Holy Grail of personal understanding it's been down the rabbit hole of "boredom" that I have discovered most promising veins of gold. Come now, I will show you.

From the old Testament we inherited a potent list of Ten Commandments. I am sure many of you learned these authoritative "shall not" rules of conduct at a young and impressionable age just as I did. They are all excellent suggestions passed down to us from a far simpler time and written for a simple people. Don't get me wrong, without a doubt your life will go smoother if you tend to follow these guidelines than if you don't. In addition, there is no way to calculate how important they have functioned in guiding humanity toward less destructive probability strands. However, I have come to realize that there actually are only two Universal Directives, above and beyond these dated commandments, which ALL BEINGS must ultimately follow. (As crazy as this might sound, I believe this even includes the Supreme Being we have termed "God.") These Universal Decrees are:

1) "KNOW THYSELF," and then,
2) "SHINE!"

It is self-evident that the Universe/Great Spirit has been "*hell-bent for leather*" (using cowboy terminology) satisfying these two universal mandates ever since the Big Bang. As I explained in "The God Process," the explosive pressure of Life to express Itself in every possible way, including as "you," is the Great Spirit's response in meeting the first of these directives. The amazing and intriguing thing to me, and critically important for you to understand, is the impossibility of satisfying this rule. Why? Again, the reason it's unattainable is because this Being is changing, growing, and evolving exponentially! This explosive exponential expansion is the logical response to probing an infinite number of possibilities, and potential variations. There is not, nor can there ever be, an end to this expansion! This is the reason in the Abraham/Hicks philosophy Abraham constantly repeats the phrase, "you'll never get it done."

I believe that the very meaning and purpose behind all Life is embedded within this eternal process of the Universe seeking to Know Itself. Another way to say this would be, the "God-Head" becoming ever more self-aware. This is the relentless force behind/beneath your feelings of boredom pushing you to expand, to become more, to seek that Yellow Brick Road of enhanced self-expression. Within you this deep impetus to grow is coming directly from the Universe relentlessly seeking Self-awareness.

Now, let's return to my original question: "Who are you?"

Answering this question is like peeling an onion. Going below the surface answers of name, occupation, nationality, race, religion, gender…. who are you really? We each must peel our own "identity onion," likely over many lifetimes, before coming to our own enlightened conclusions and realizations. For me, the obvious place to focus upon this essential question is within the mystery called "Life."

As a lad growing up I must confess that I killed many innocent living things. Give a young boy a magnifying glass, a sunny day, an anthill, and something's going to fry! Disgusting, I know, but such was the state of my boyhood LOC back then. How many helpless worms have I put on hooks, how many fish have I whacked over the head after reeling them in? Earlier I described the difficulty I had in learning to hunt squirrels on our small farm. What I didn't expand upon was how deadly efficient I eventually became when I finally learned the skills of a hunter. I became a virtual "squirrel assassin." I still recall holding those warm, limp bodies in my hand, looking down in awe and wonder at the stark contrast between being so alive, just a moment ago, and now dead. I was both enthralled and mystified by this thing called life. What was it? How did this vital force infuse the clay of matter with "squirrel-ness," or me with my "boy-ness?"

Previously I explained how the many years I labored obtaining advanced degrees in Life Science did little to answer these questions. The one conclusion I did come away with during those years of cutting and dicing apart all types of organic specimens during my biology labs was that there was a single Life energy. The energy flowing through even the lowly bacteria and myself had to be the same. This certainly had to be the case if the evolution story was correct. This one living energy probed and pushed into ever more complex and adaptive forms through billions of years. This was the clear and unmistakable message written in stone of the fossil record. Although this fact of there being but one Life Force flowing through all the varied forms may seem boringly obvious to some readers, it was a profound realization for me. This was the unspoken beautiful and profound message behind the misunderstood and much-maligned theory of evolution. <u>We are all vibrant expressions of this One Life seeking expression.</u>

So, "Who are you?" It should now be obvious that "you" are not just a vibrating hive of trillions of cells called a "body." You literally ARE this One Life Force flowing within and through that vibrating horde of cells. You ARE that blue burning flame! Numerous "after death" books in recent years reaffirm over and again the ongoing vitality of your personal energy or "soul" after being declared physically dead. Yes, the form of you, your beloved body, will dissolve, but not the energy. A metaphor that helped me understand this flow of Life/Spirit energy, compared to what I think of as my "soul," is the particle versus wave paradox of light.

The nature of light mystified science for many years. Light reacted in a totally opposite manner depending on how it was examined. In doing this, light appeared to be either made up of either discrete packets or flowing waves. It all depended upon how you experimentally examined it. This is very confusing because then light seems to be able to manifest in two radically different ways at the same time. Regardless, in either form, it is still light. Likewise, the Life Force flowing through us can appear to be as separate packets (bodies) or a flowing wave (Spirit). Just as in the nature of light, both views are valid and thus paradoxical. The important point is realizing that in essence YOU simply ARE this Life Force, this flowing, expanding energy.

The first Universal directive is now answered. You know what you are, this One Life pushing forth within a fleshy form. Now, the next logical question is, *"What should you do?"* The answer is to follow, as best you can, the second Universal Rule for all beings, great and small, and SHINE!

Most of us have been raised believing that physical survival, in the most comfortable manner, is the primary focus of life. Now you can see how this comes about from a total misconception of who, or what, you really are. This underlying "comfortable survival at all costs" focus of life only makes sense if you have bought into the belief of being merely a fragile, ephemeral, physical body. Now you know better. You know who you really are: the unending, unique expression of the Great Spirit of Life unfolding, becoming MORE. <u>This realization changes everything</u>! You, and every other living thing are part of a massive, unending, upwelling living energy seeking Self-Knowledge and Self-Expression! Now, do you see why you no longer require those Ten Commandments? Do you really need to be told not to steal from yourself or kill another aspect of "you?" Would not all days be holy? What could you possibly "covet" when you know all is yours in the first place? All you want to do once you realize your true identity is SHINE, just like the magnificent Universe you're an integral part of.

The question deep within you - within all of us - is, *"How should I shine?"* The whole point of this book has been outlining how to use the power hidden beneath your boredom to guide you toward your shining path of self-expression. The Spirit of this One Life ever seeks to grow, to shine as it eternally attempts to more fully know ITs expanding Self. Following the breadcrumb signs from the Universe you will be led to your path, your Way, to your greater yet to be. Most of us know of some individuals who have a distinctive glow about them. It is obvious they are in love with life and express this loving energy in everything they do. These people are on their path and they are shining.

Again, it is through living your Tao that you shine. To grow, to discover, to take part in this great enterprise of eternal self-discovery is your destiny. The famous theoretical physicist, Stephen Hawking is someone who is obviously upon his Tao-path. In the book, A New Earth by Eckhart Tolle, a quote by Hawking beautifully encapsulated the radiant attitude of one who is shining when he said of his life, *"Who could ask for more?"*

CHAPTER 15

Let It Be!

"The Source that you've become is available to
you at all times if you will but let It be."
ABRAHAM/HICKS

At this point I hope you have a firm grasp of this amazing power hidden behind the feelings of boredom. You should understand that the power of which I am speaking is not just some power, but all power. It is the power behind and within the expanding Universe and the exponentially expanding Godhead Itself. It is the Power of creation that knows no limits and is perpetuating and enhancing Itself right here, right now, as YOU!

Feelings of boredom and discontent emanate from within you, from your very soul, when you are off your personal path. There exists deep within each of us the silent knowledge of this path or Way. You know it's there, waiting for your steps with the same certainty that you know your name. Each of us have come from the factory, like cosmic radios, tuned to the frequency of our personal good. Because of this you can never escape from the inner knowing and longing to be on your Way.

As a hunter of your Yellow Brick Road, you will never cease stalking along pathways toward an ever-greater good. We are all green, vibrant vines of potentialities, of frisky probabilities, seeking the Light. For countless reasons our lives go astray and we wander off into the dark, rocky regions. This causes something deep within our souls to cry out for the Light. I have termed this soulful ache for our MORE "boredom." It was assumed this state was just a personal problem only to be solved through efforts of the affected individual alone. Unfortunately, these efforts often tend only to make the situation worse by seeking ever-greater distractions and ways to waste personal power. In this book my goal is to shatter this notion of having private discontent and provide a means for regaining your pathway in the Light. Your ache for MORE is not yours alone but that of the eternally expanding Spirit within.

Once in a dream, during my struggles to understand all of this, I slowly drifted awake hearing the Beatles song, "Let it be," playing in my head (soul?). As I slowly came toward the surface I first took this as meaning, "All is well, cease struggling." This was no doubt true and had a nice, motherly feeling. Then things got loud. Suddenly, the softness of the Beatle's song was gone and the gentle advice to simply "let it be" transformed into a booming imperative command, "LET IT BE!" Sitting straight up in bed, with the words ringing in my head, I slowly understood.

Previously I mentioned that the term "IT" is the one I often use for what others call "God." The word "God" simply has too much attached baggage for me. Calling this ineffable, creative Being "IT" has just seemed more appropriate to me personally. What I finally understood hearing the authoritative command to "LET IT BE!" ringing in my head was this:

"Quit thinking so small! You are a consciousness probe of the expanding Infinite, of the magnificent Universe! WAKE UP! Quit limiting yourself. When you do, you limit ME. Let Me be MORE through you! *Let the Universe become MORE by finding The Way, your Tao. Rise above your timidity and fear. Pay attention! Follow, follow, follow the signs ever given along your Yellow Brick Road. LET US BECOME!"*

CHAPTER 16

Synopsis

*"Like sands through an hourglass, these
are the days of our lives."*
DAYS OF OUR LIVES, T.V. SERIES

t has been a long and interesting trail from those days squirrel hunting back in the rich hardwood forests of Kentucky. Little did I know then how far those early morning lessons on waiting and stalking would take me along my Way.

Spiritual wisdom is a hard-won commodity. It takes time. It takes many mistakes. For me it has also taken long stretches of waiting, periods of intense boredom punctuated by flashes of insight, scattered miracles, and occasional moments of tearful joy. Looking back now upon this long, convoluted trail, I am sobered by my innocent stupidity as I blundered headstrong and clueless for so many precious years. Is it even possible to help anyone avoid these inefficient blunderings off the path? At times I am struck by feelings of the futility expressed in the precious book, _Siddhartha_, by Hermann Hesse when he stated that, "wisdom is incommunicable." Yet, perhaps it's possible for words, of sufficient power and impact, to act as a sharp, polished plow, turning the soil of the soul in preparation for green sprouts of understanding come spring.

"Time," my friends, is the problem. You are running out of time. We all are. When this truth is allowed to sink in you realize you can't afford to live the unconscious, reckless, inefficient life you have been living any longer! The biggest hazard to all of us, especially hunters of The Way stalking probabilities, is the subconscious belief of having plenty of time to figure this all out. You don't! We have all been mesmerized by the adolescent mindset of a TV culture projecting the belief that illness, old age, and death are just things that happen to the unfortunate. If we just eat right, take our vitamins, and exercise then we have nothing to worry about: "go back to sleep."

Since you have only a limited amount of time it simply makes sense that you spend it efficiently. Following your Way, your Tao, your Yellow Brick Road, is really the best way to live an efficient life full to the brim of joy, power and creative expression. It is only when we have made a deep connection with Spirit and then follow Its guidance toward our MORE that this will occur. Our feelings of boredom with some aspect of our lives are the alarm bells indicating this is not happening. These feelings must not be ignored or indulged, but instead used as motivation to be unwavering hunters of our sacred path. Anything else is just wasting our very precious time.

To hunt for your path, your Yellow Brick Road, you must be able to wait as the power behind your boredom builds and the Universe signals what to do. Most people waste this power of boredom through countless distractions and indulgences. The waiting of a hunter is an act of faith that the expanding Spirit of the Universe will not ignore. While waiting, the hunter maintains a high level of consciousness remaining ever alert for intuitive ideas and external signals. When these ideas or signals come, the hunter acts boldly, yet remains unattached to outcomes. Both successful moves and mistaken ones are used to build the hunter's faith in their connection with Spirit. You, as a hunter of your good, must be ever poised to make both small and large moves following Spirit's guidance. Over time, as your Spirit-power increases, your ability to see your Way will grow. As a dedicated hunter of your sacred path you will also develop a strong inner sense of timing. More and more you will find yourself in the right place at the right time, for both your good and that of others. This personal dance with Spirit becomes the ongoing joy of the resolute hunter. The boredom, or dissatisfaction of the past fades to a distant memory.

In your life the absolutely essential skills are being able to wait upon, see, and then follow the signs from the Universe/Spirit. Everything else is secondary. Your hunter's alertness developed over time, from sensing the subtle feelings of boredom and also those wisps of joy, allows you to navigate steadily along your path, your Way. As you steadfastly follow this path of MORE, you will continually deepen your understanding of just who you really are, and how to best SHINE your unique frequency of Spirit's Light. Your singular job is to LET IT BE expressed through your life, ever anew, along the eternal, luminous Way.

"In expressing Itself through us, It becomes
more fully conscious of Its own being."
ERNEST HOLMES

CHAPTER 17

A review of my "New Conclusions"

"You are a vibrational being who has come forth from Source Energy. You are a creator and knew that your best creating is done out there on the leading edge where there are all of these magnificent choices to choose from. Why? For the purpose of coming to new conclusions."

ABRAHAM/HICKS

- Feelings of boredom and dissatisfaction are not to be avoided or indulged in. Instead, you should appreciate and recognize these feelings as indicators your life is off course.

- Boredom is the sign there is MORE waiting for you and that the expanding Universe is seeking harmonious expansion through you.

- The Universe is alive, awake, and aware. It wants to communicate with you and express more Life through you.

- "God" is actually the eternal PROCESS of Life/Spirit learning, becoming more, and not some completed, judgmental Being "up in heaven."

- The purpose or meaning of Life is the expansion of awareness. The Intent of the Great Spirit within all Life is to explore and express Its infinitely growing potential.

- This Spirit seeks to expand along pathways of symmetry, beauty, and harmony called the "Tao."

- Your personal Tao, your "Yellow Brick Road" of beautiful, joyful expansion, IS NOW and awaits your footsteps.

- To find your way back upon your path, your Yellow Brick Road, you must think and act as an intensely alert, yet patient hunter.

- Hunters know how to wait, allowing the power beneath their boredom to build. They know why they are waiting: for the Power to see The Way. They know what they are waiting for: signs and signals from Spirit guiding them.

- Hunters of Power move slowly, carefully, conserving their energy, ever alert for these signs and signals.

- Hunters of The Way keep a close watch on their thoughts and level of consciousness. They realize their habitual thoughts will either empower or deplete them.

- Hunters along their path to a more abundant Life understand the importance of probabilities; therefore, they are very careful with their choices and actions. They know their time is limited and don't waste it wandering along fruitless trails.

- Hunters stalking their path are free of attachments and addictions. They know they must remain clearheaded and light-footed to hear and follow the whispered guidance of Spirit.

- When the time to move and act comes, the patient hunter moves swiftly and efficiently without hesitation or fear.

- Hunter-stalkers of The Way are not afraid to make mistakes. They know how to learn from their wrong moves, and have faith Spirit will always guide them back to the trail.

- The feelings of both boredom and curiosity are the result of our spirit being part of the Great expanding Spirit of the Universe. In truth we are but root tips of this growing Spirit of Infinity seeking Self-knowledge and ever more beautiful ways to SHINE.

- The joy of the Tao hunter is, moment-by-moment, seeing and following Spirit, allowing IT to become more, along their Yellow Brick Road.

"Something hidden.
Go and find it.
Go and look behind the Ranges --
Something lost behind the Ranges.
Lost and waiting for you.
Go!"
R. KIPLING

References

Bellow, Saul. *The Adventures of Augie March.* Viking Press, New York. 1953

Bible References. *The English Standard Version Bible.* New York: Oxford University Press, 2009.

Burroughs, John. *The Little Book of American Poets: 1787-1900.* Ed. Jessie B. Rittenhouse. Cambridge: Riverside Press, 1915.

Byrne, Rhonda. *The Secret.* Beyond Words Publishing, New York, 2006

Castaneda, Carlos. *The Teachings of Don Juan: A Yaqui Way of Knowledge.* Berkeley: University of California Press, 1998

Carey, Ken. *Return of the Bird Tribes.* Talman Company, Inc. New York, 1998

Goldsmith, Joel S. *The Infinite Way.* BN Publishing. U.S.A. 2007

Hesse, Hermann. *Siddhartha.* New Directions and Bantam Publishing. New York, 1971

Hicks, Esther and Jerry. *The Law of Attraction: The Basics of the Teachings of Abraham.* Hay House, 2006

Hicks, Esther and Jerry. *The Law of Attraction Workshop*, San Rafael, CA. February 2008

Hill, Napoleon; Cornwell, Ross. *Think and Grow Rich!* San Diego, CA: Aventine Press, 2004

Holmes, Ernest. *This Thing Called Life.* G.P. Putnam's Sons Publishers, New York, 1943

Holmes, Ernest. *The Science of Mind.* Dodd, Mead and Company, New York, 1938

Kipling, Rudyard. *The Explorer.* Collected Verse of Rudyard Kipling. Doubleday, Page and Co. 1915

McTaggart, Lynne. *The Field.* HarperCollins Publishers, New York, 2002

Mulford, Prentice. *Thoughts are Things & The God In You.* Wilder Publications, Radford, VA. 2008

Peale, Norman Vincent. *The Power of Positive Thinking.* Prentice-Hall, Inc. New York, 1952

Roberts, Jane, *Psychic Politics.* Prentice-Hall, Inc. New Jersey, 1976

Thoreau, Henry David. *Walden.* Princeton University Press, 2004

Tolle, Eckhart. *The Power of Now.* Namaste Publishing and New World Library, Novato, California, 1999

Tolle, Eckhart. *A New Earth: Awakening to your Life's Purpose.* Namaste Publishing, Vancouver, British Columbia, Canada, 2005

Troward, Thomas. *Edinburgh Lectures on Mental Science*. Dodd, Mead and Company, New York 1909.

Weiss M.D., Brian. *Many Lives, Many Masters*. Simon & Schuster Inc., 1988